Single- and twin-seater Sukhoi Su-17 "Fitter" ground attack fighters with their crews.

EAST VERSUS WEST

B8–Wombat
In the snows of Norway, Bv202 tracked snow vehicle fitted with British 120-mm Wombat antitank gun.

EAST VERSUS WEST

LESLIE McDONNELL

GALLERY BOOKS
An Imprint of W. H. Smith Publishers Inc.
112 Madison Avenue
New York City 10016

High above the North Atlantic a USAF F-4 Phantom II pilot tracks a Soviet Tupolev Tu-95 Bear 4-D on a reconnaissance mission. Even in peace NATO remains alert, ready to counter any threat.

This book was devised and produced by
Multimedia Publications (UK) Ltd.

Editor: Andie Oppenheimer
Production: Karen Bromley
Design: Brian Harris
Picture Research: The Research House

First published in the United States of America 1986 by
Gallery Books, an imprint of W.H. Smith Publishers Inc.,
112 Madison Avenue, New York, NY 10016.

ISBN 0 8317 2578 8

Typeset by Tradespools Limited
Origination by Wace Group PLC
Printed by Cayfosa, Barcelona, Spain.

Contents

NATO v Warsaw Pact

The Power Blocs

War, it is often said, no matter where or when it is fought, is governed less by expediency than by lessons learnt from a previous war. Certainly World War III, if ever the dread event comes about – and President Nixon as long ago as 1980 claimed it was already being fought in South and Central America, South East Asia and the Middle East – will owe much of its background to the lessons learnt and the fears arising from World War II.

The great divide between East and West, which seems to be a permanent feature of the modern world, can only be fully understood after looking at the respective histories of the communist and capitalist blocs. Because of these, a war that would be regarded as legitimate by Washington, Bonn or London, is often seen as "aggressive" by Moscow, where Lenin's doctrine of what is a "just war" still prevails. Likewise, the attack launched by North Korea against its neighbor South Korea in 1950 was justified in communist terms because it spread socialist ideology to an allegedly oppressed people.

How they came about

"What will be the position in a year or two when the British and American armies have melted away and the French have not yet been formed on any major scale and when Russia may choose to keep 200 or 300 divisions on active service?" "An iron curtain is drawn down upon their (the Russian) front. We do not know what is going on behind . . ." Telegram from Churchill to Truman, May 1945.

The Warsaw Pact did not come into existence until 1955, several years after the formation of the North Atlantic Treaty Organization (NATO). In fact, the Soviet Union exercised such tight control over the Eastern bloc by the autumn of 1945 that a formal alliance was unnecessary. In liberating Eastern Europe from fascism during 1944 and 1945, Moscow took pains to fill the void left by the fleeing Germans with a carefully controlled domestic government of its own choosing. In the case of Poland,

Right: The "Big Three Conference", Potsdam, August 1945. Seated (left to right) are the British Prime Minister Attlee, US President Truman and the Soviet leader Stalin. The intention was to discuss the division of post-war Europe, but by that time the Russians already controlled most of Eastern Europe.

Inset: The Soviets during and after the war expanded their empire, in terms of both population and land. Only Yugoslavia did not accept their leadership. Albania left the Soviet fold in the early 1960s.

1940 – 1948
k²
1940 0,5 45.600
1940 1,1 47.700
1940 2,0 64.700
1940 3,0 59.600
1945 1,2 13.500
1945 11,8 181.300
1945 0,7 12.700
1945 3,7 50.200
24,0 475 300
1945 18,8 111.100
1945 26,5 311.700
1948 12,3 127.900
1947 9,8 93.000
1948 16,1 237.200
1946 7,2 110.800
1946 1,2 27.500
91,9 1.019.200

Left: West Berliners stare at the "iron curtain" that descended on their city in 1961, a permanent reminder of the deep divisions and suspicions that exist between East and West.

The Berlin airlift, 1948. A Douglas C-54 Skymaster of the USAF Air Transport Command flies in supplies to West Berlin after the Soviets had blockaded the isolated city.

Above: The countries who signed the North Atlantic Treaty on 4 April 1949 were, in alphabetical order (here numbered 1–12): Belgium, Canada, Denmark, France, Iceland, Italy, Luxembourg, the Netherlands, Norway, Portugal, the UK and the USA. They were joined by Greece (13) and Turkey (14) in 1952, the Federal Republic of Germany in 1955, and Spain in 1982.

the Free Polish Government that had taken refuge in London was ignored. Instead, Polish prisoners of war, stripped of their officers and NCOs, were formed into two new armies (the "Wojsko Polskie") to spearhead the liberation of Poland and at the same time to usher in a communist regime. In Romania, Bulgaria and Hungary, all of whom had collaborated with the Nazis, the job was made that much easier. Fervent communists who had fought fascism in their own country, such as Gottwald in Czechoslovakia and Ulbricht in East Germany, were used to implement the Soviet rule. Where none were available, Moscow simply granted one of its own citizens dual nationality and promoted him as leader of the satellite state. By the beginning of 1946, the Soviet Union had complete mastery of the satellite countries within the Eastern bloc and had stationed there large elements of its four-million-strong army.

While the Soviet Union had retained its armies at virtual war-strength after the war, Western Europe had demobilized to such an extent that, collectively, it could raise no more than 20 divisions. Alarmed at this imbalance, and realizing the growing need for economic cooperation, the UK, France and the Benelux countries signed a treaty of mutual assistance in the spring of 1948. This was followed by a wider Brussels Treaty which included the original signatories as well as the United States, Canada, Denmark, Italy, Iceland and Portugal.

In Washington on April 4, 1949, all the countries who had signed the Brussels Treaty ratified what became known as the North Atlantic Treaty Organization. By this, they agreed articles strictly within the Charter of the United Nations, undertaking to promote the economic and financial well-being of all constituent parties, and reaffirming the principles of collective defense should any member be threatened within the sphere of NATO's influence.

Significantly, the treaty did not offer mutual assistance to a constituent country who – for any reason whatsoever – found itself at war in the southern hemisphere or the Far East. Thus, when the UK tried to fulfill what it considered to be its post-colonial responsibilities in Malaya, Kenya and Borneo, it turned not to NATO for help but to its Commonwealth partners. Likewise, Korea was a United Nations rather than NATO conflict, as was Vietnam.

Six years after the formation of NATO, the Warsaw Pact or, more correctly, the Warsaw Treaty Organization, was signed on May 14 1955. The signatories included the Soviet Union, Albania (no longer a member), Bulgaria, Czechoslovakia, East Germany, Hungary, Poland and Romania. Thus were formed the two power blocs that have governed East-West relations and dominated the world political arena ever since.

The Modern Alliances

NATO

In 1951, the twelve original NATO signatories invited Greece and Turkey to join them. Both did so a year later, more out of fear of each other than of Eastern bloc communism. For reasons of political expediency, West Germany was admitted as a member in 1955. From the start, member states tended to concentrate more on the security aspects of the treaty rather than on its economic and social potential.

In 1966, France withdrew from NATO's Integrated Military Command Structure so as to enable the French to retain total control of their own defense planning, but remained a formal member of NATO, contributing fully to the North Atlantic Council. France's nuclear deterrent is geared to the principle of "flexible response" (*la riposte graduée*), similar to that of the rest of the Alliance, and no one seriously doubts that the well-equipped French armed forces would play a full role in the event of any future hostilities in Europe.

NATO has been aptly described as a free association of sovereign states and, as such, ensures that every member is consulted fully in its policy-making. Although the United States predominates militarily, it accepts that it must give full consideration to the views of its European allies who, being much closer to the potential threat of the Soviet Union, often see their priorities very differently.

NATO's command structure

Direction at the highest level comes from the North Atlantic Council, structured upon the principles of a national cabinet. The Council meets twice yearly at foreign ministerial level, but is in permanent session at ambassadorial level, in Evère, near Brussels. The Council oversees various committees dealing with such diverse topics as defense, external affairs, finance, construction, communications and planning. It has its own Chiefs-of-Staff Committee (known usually as the Military

Committee), with its own internal structure for dealing with plans, logistics, communications and standardization. Most importantly, the chairman of the Military Committee is responsible for ensuring that the Defense Planning Committee, which itself meets regularly at ambassadorial and ministerial levels, is aware of the collective view of the allied military chiefs-of-staff, and that the Military Committee takes note of the views of the Council on all matters. France has no seat on the Defense Planning Committee, but does have a limited voice on the Military Committee and is in many respects treated as a fully committed member. This crucial, and usually friction-free, link between the politicans and the military is really the cornerstone of NATO democracy.

The Secretary-General, presently Lord Carrington of the UK, is the most powerful figure within the Alliance, with responsibility

Left: US troops firing a 4.2-inch mortar on enemy positions during the Korean war. Korea saw the US and her Allies, under the flag of the United Nations , combine to face the Communists with a unity of purpose that has not been seen since.

Below: Single- and twin-seater Sukhoi Su-17 "Fitter" ground attack fighters with their crews. They are typical of the force available to the Soviet Frontal Aviation to support any action against NATO.

for co-ordinating all economic and military committees. Several important agencies, such as the Military Committee for Standardization, based in Evère, the Advisory Group for Aerospace Research and Development in Paris, and the NATO Defense College in Rome, are also under his charge.

The forces assigned to the Alliance, which by no means constitute the member countries' entire armed forces, are placed under the control of one of three commanders. The Supreme Allied Commander Europe (SACEUR) is based in Mons, some 40 miles (60 km) from Council Headquarters at Evère. SACEUR is always a United States General who also assumes the role of Commander-in-Chief United States Forces in Europe (CINCUSEUR). The Supreme Allied Commander Atlantic (SACLANT) is based in Norfolk, Virginia, USA, and is a United States Admiral. The Commander-in-Chief Channel (CINCCHAN), based at Northwood, on the outskirts of London, UK, is a British admiral who combines the post with that of Commander-in-Chief (British) Fleet.

Because SACEUR evolved from the original USA-UK-France link there is a danger that it will always be regarded as superior to SACLANT, while CINCCHAN will invariably be seen as little more than a sop to British ego. To ensure that unnecessary and potentially harmful domestic squabbles are kept to a minimum, the staffs throughout are integrated as far as possible. SACEUR itself is divided into three subordinate commands. Allied Forces

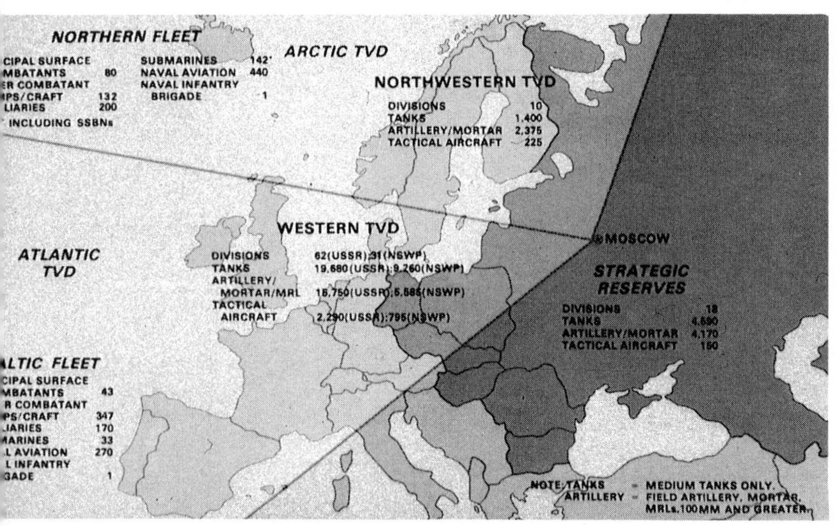

Northern Europe (AFNORTH) is based in Kolsas, Norway, and takes responsibility for the protection of Scandinavia from the Arctic wastes of Northern Norway to Schleswig-Holstein, Northern Germany. The area is bounded by neutral Sweden and Finland and by the Soviet Union, and is lightly populated. AFNORTH relies upon the speedy arrival of highly trained specialist reinforcements, such as the British Royal Marine Commandos, for protection from both the Soviet Army and the two Soviet fleets based in the White Sea and the Baltic, together with the combined navies of Poland and East Germany.

Allied Forces Southern Europe (AFSOUTH), based in Naples, is responsible for the security of the Mediterranean. This rather complex command contains more troops than the rest of NATO combined, mainly because Greece and Turkey both maintain large standing armies as a defense against each other, rather than against the Warsaw Pact. Both countries rely heavily upon obsolete equipment, donated or purchased second-hand, and neither is politically reliable. Consequently, the once

Left: To ensure the effective use of all forces and weapons, the Soviets bring them together under a unified command for each theater of military operations (TVD). This map shows the size of the forces facing NATO in northern and central Europe and in the Atlantic.

omnipotent US Sixth Fleet is now threatened in the Mediterranean by the ever-growing and very modern Soviet Fifth Fleet. However, the presence of a powerful French navy, which could come to the aid of NATO in the event of war, must not be discounted.

Most important of all is Allied Forces Central (AFCENT), based at Brunssum, Netherlands. This is the command that would expect to bear the brunt of any Warsaw Pact offensive. It consists of the bulk of the allied forces in Western Germany, divided into two army groups, NORTHAG and CENTAG, and

Left: One of the elite bodies of the Soviet armed forces, the KGB, some of whom are seen here in East Berlin for one of the regular military parades, recruits only the best and most loyal conscripts to its ranks.

Above: As an alliance of sovereign states, Nato relies on cooperation between the armed forces of member countries. Here, an American marine briefs colleagues from other NATO states.

two tactical air forces, 2nd ATAF and 4th ATAF. The recently formed ACE Mobile Force (AMF), with its emphasis on an airborne response, is also available to SACEUR.

Allied Command Atlantic (ACLANT) takes responsibility for the defense of the Atlantic Ocean from the North Pole to the Tropic of Cancer, and has the unenviable task of ensuring that at least local superiority is maintained while United States reserves cross to Europe. It is divided into six sub-commands, three geographical (Western Atlantic, Eastern Atlantic and Iberian Atlantic) and three functional (Striking Fleet Atlantic, Submarine Command and Standing Naval Force Atlantic).

Warsaw Pact

The Warsaw Pact, or Warsaw Treaty Organization, is fundamentally different from NATO. It was signed as a matter of procedure by the Soviet Union and her various satellites in 1955, and only Albania, with its own peculiar brand of fundamental communism, has been allowed to resign from it, though the loyalty of Romania must be suspect. None of the intricate subcommittees to be found within NATO exist in the Warsaw Pact, which is under the absolute control of the Soviet Union. Tactics, training and the vast majority of military equipment are Soviet, but there is a growing tendency for certain items to be produced under license in the satellite countries.

Air defense is totally centralized under the command of a single Soviet Deputy Commander, who takes full responsibility for the six main air defense districts within the Pact, and for the 10 districts within the Soviet Union itself. Individual Pact members are responsible for the air defense of their own skies,

Left: Responsible for an area reaching from the cold of the Arctic to the warmth of the Mediterranean, SACEUR can call on the US Marines to support any operations on NATO's flanks. Here, three marines wait in the snows of Norway, armed with M16s. The one on the right has an M203 grenade launcher.

Above: In Vietnam the US fought a war without any military or at times political support from its European allies. Here, a US Skyraider drops napalm on enemy territory.

Left: Within the communist bloc Yugoslavia was never part of the Warsaw Pact and has always followed its own independent foreign policy. Here a Yugoslav sniper takes aim, echoing the role of his partisan forefathers who fought as partisans against the Fascists during World War II.

Right: Stretching from the northern cape of Norway to the Mediterranean, and from the Atlantic to the eastern borders of Turkey, Allied Command Europe (ACE) is subdivided into three subordinate commands, AFNORTH, AFCENT and AFSOUTH. Supreme Headquarters Allied Powers Europe (SHAPE) is based near Mons in Belgium.

Bottom: After the Soviet invasion of 1968, the Czechoslovak services remain firmly part of the Warsaw Pact and can field 10 divisions. Among their armory is the Czech-designed and built M53/59 Twin 30-mm AA SP gun system.

but the single commander has absolute mastery of all fighter/interceptor aircraft, all radar and electronic warfare equipment and all SAM sites dedicated to air defense.

Soviet Missions, based in each capital and staffed entirely by Soviet officers, ensure that as far as possible the various armies of the Warsaw Pact remain a single cohesive fighting force, while attachés, stationed at each embassy and legation, maintain political reliability. The KGB, sometimes aided by domestic resources provided by the more reliable allies, notably East Germany, are in charge of all matters of security, including the physical security of the Soviet border. Thus, while the so-called "inner German border" between East and West Germany is guarded by East German soldiers, that between Poland and the Soviet Union is guarded by hand-picked KGB members of the elite border guard, equipped with their own armor, artillery and logistics.

The Soviet Union is the sole nuclear power within the Warsaw Pact and shows no inclination to relinquish this position. She has, however, been "invited" by certain of her satellites to station nuclear weapons on their soil. Not surprisingly, the East Germans and Czechs were far less vocal in their objections to the installation of SS-20 missiles on their territory than the West Germans, British, Italians or Dutch who protested against cruise missiles.

The Soviet Union has always provided most of the front-line forces and now has over 30 "Category A" divisions forward. These are divided into four "Groups of Soviet Forces", based in East Germany, Poland, Czechoslovakia and Hungary. Non-Soviet forces are divided into a "Northern tier" comprising East Germany, Poland and Czechoslovakia and a "Southern tier" of Hungary, Bulgaria and Romania.

Attitudes between the Soviet soldier and his Warsaw Pact host vary considerably from country to country, as does the percentage of gross national product allocated by each member to its own defense.

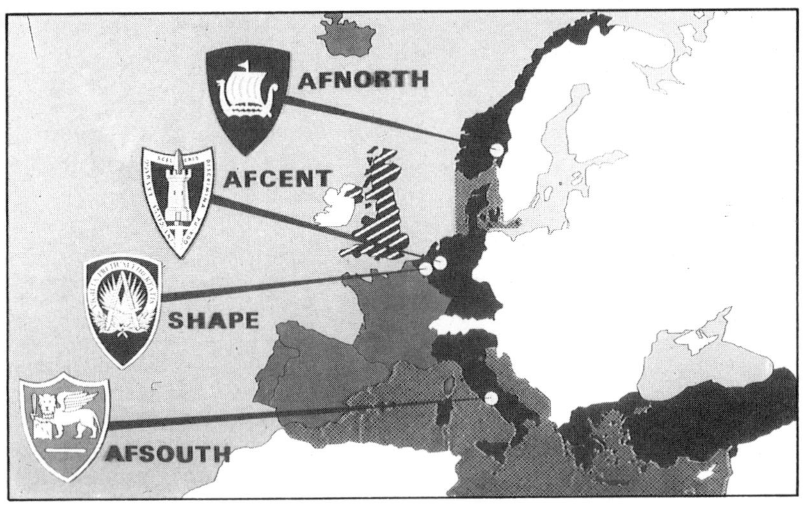

Eastern Europe

East German forces comprise four motor-rifle divisions and two tank divisions. They are highly motivated, well-equipped and considered by the Soviets to be their most reliable ally. Charged with the responsibility of guarding the most sensitive of all borders, the East Germans also provide a very modern coastal navy and special forces (the Willi Staengar Battalion in particular) second to none within the Warsaw Pact.

Entente, however, is often no more than skin deep. For although every town in East Germany contains a monument to those of the Red Army who gave their lives in its liberation from fascism, and huge placards welcoming the Russian "protectors" abound, both Soviet and German youth are reared on stories of wartime atrocities committed by the other and a deep and mutual feeling of distrust remains. The Soviet soldier is not encouraged to mix socially with his usually more affluent German counterpart and barracks are strictly segregated. Soviet officers and non-commissioned officers, stationed in Germany for between two and five years, are forced to commute a sizable portion of their income until their return to the Soviet Union and thus are often unable to exploit the much higher standard of consumer goods on sale in cities such as Berlin and Dresden.

Poland boasts the largest non-Soviet army, with five tank divisions, five motor-rifle divisions, one airborne and one amphibious division. Morale, however, has been severely undermined during the course of the last decade and, while the army could be relied upon to defend the homeland valiantly, its value in a war of territorial aggression must be in doubt. To add to their dilemma, the Soviets are fearful that the numerous supply lines passing through Poland might be liable to sabotage should the Soviet military grip ever be released.

The position with regard to Czechoslovakia remains uncertain. The army has now largely recovered from the shattering effects of the 1968 invasion, and indeed now comprises five tank and five motor-rifle divisions and an airborne regiment. Nevertheless, resentment runs deep and the Soviets have had to make many economic concessions to help ease the situation. Soviet propaganda tries to assure the outside world that Czechoslovakia has now returned willingly to the

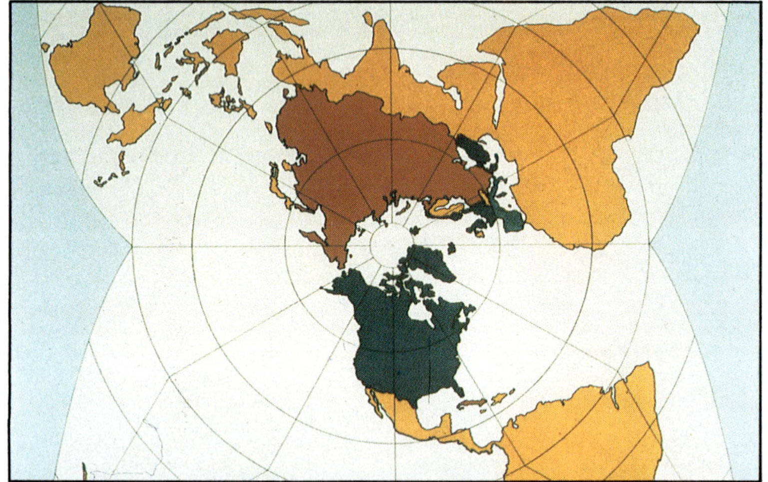

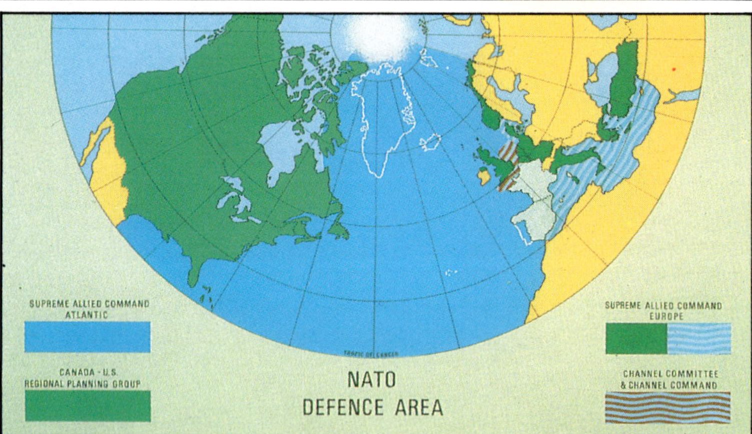

Top: Map of the northern hemisphere showing the NATO countries (green) and Warsaw Pact (brown). From its point of view, the USSR is surrounded by North America, Europe, China and Japan, all hostile, with a long, inhospitable border and the Indian sub-continent to the south. But reinforcement for the Warsaw Pact is easier than for NATO, which is divided by the vast Atlantic Ocean.

Above: There are three major NATO commanders responsible for its defence: Supreme Allied Commander Europe (SACEUR), Supreme Allied Commander Atlantic (SACLANT) and Commander-in-Chief Channel (CINCHAN). A Regional Planning Group covers the defense of the North American continent.

The aircraft carrier USS *America* underway with her Battle Group. Sixteen aircraft from a carrier air wing fly ahead – an example of the resources that SACLANT has under command to keep the North Atlantic sealanes open.

Bottom left: US troops, after crossing the Atlantic by Lockheed C-141 Starlifter, assemble at Luxembourg Airport on one of the regular reinforcement exercises.

communist fold. But it must be noted that there is now a large Soviet force stationed in Czechoslovakia where, prior to the invasion, there was no military presence at all.

In certain respects, the situations of the "Southern tier" of the Warsaw Pact and the southern flank of NATO are similar. Hungary and Bulgaria, like Greece and Turkey, both maintain large armies though neither is up to strength or modern enough to present a serious threat to a well-prepared enemy. Romania has a sizable army of two tank and eight motor-rifle divisions, three mountain and one airborne brigades, but is otherwise badly equipped and is even turning to the West for new equipment. No Soviet troops are billeted on Romanian soil. Romania has a treaty of mutual defense with Yugoslavia and it is quite possible that Romania will continue to move away from the influence of the Warsaw Pact, preferring to join her neighbor as a well-defended neutral.

Unlike NATO, the Warsaw Pact as an alliance would cease in time of war, its various armies coming under the direct control of Soviet marshals. How willingly large elements of it would fight a war of Soviet aggression remains unknown. Without a concerted propaganda effort prior to any conflict, it would be difficult to motivate most of the satellites.

How they compare

Any comparison of the two Alliances must take into account not only military capabilities but also other factors such as political and social stability, geography and technological resourcefulness. Both the United States and Soviet Union have global responsibilities and both maintain substantial forces in Asia and the Pacific. But whereas the United States could almost certainly, without danger, reduce its forces in an emergency, for the Soviet Union to do so would mean leaving its long border with China undefended. To make matters worse, the Soviets are now embroiled in Afghanistan, and cannot in the conceivable future reduce their forces there to below 100,000 without suffering a defeat which could have strong repercussions among her growing Moslem minority. The Warsaw Pact, however, has the advantage of being a single geographical entity, unlike NATO, which is separated by oceans, seas and, in the southern flank, potentially hostile territory. It can thus transport men and supplies relatively easily and securely. The Soviet Navy, however, suffers the disadvantage of operating from four widely spread areas of deployment, three of which run the danger of potential blockade.

NATO suffers severely from problems of resupply and must rely heavily upon shipping to transport men and equipment from the United States. An increasing amount of its mercantile tonnage is now sailing under neutral "flags of convenience" which will not always be available in an emergency. NATO has dangerously little territorial depth in Europe, with the result that supplies, once landed, will be constantly vulnerable to attack from the growing Soviet tactical air force. The necessity for keeping open the sea lanes has resulted in a strong bias towards antisubmarine warfare, so that many of NATO's smaller ships would now be totally defenseless against concerted air attack. The highly professional Royal Navy suffered heavily at the hands of the Argentine Air Force in the South Atlantic in 1982 because of this paucity of effective air defense, but losses would have been far worse if more of the bombs that found their targets had exploded.

The Warsaw Pact has over seven million men under arms, including a million or so in internal security forces like the KGB, but only about four million actually face NATO in Europe. World-wide, Warsaw Pact active and reserve forces include 246 divisions plus 29 specialist brigades, over 61,000 main battle

NATO ARMED FORCES

Country	Population	Conscription Period (months)	Armed Forces	Conscripts	Conscripts as % Armed Forces	Armed Forces as % Total Population
Greece	10,200,000	22–26	178,000	137,000	76.97	1.75
Turkey	48,600,000	20	602,000	544,000	90.37	1.24
Belgium	9,900,000	8–10	93,607	31,908	34.09	0.95
USA	236,700,000	Nil	2,135,900	Nil	Nil	0.90
Norway	4,146,000	12–15	36,785	22,500	61.17	0.89
France	54,600,000	12	471,350	244,900	51.96	0.86
Spain	38,800,000	15	330,000	214,000	64.85	0.85
Germany	61,400,000	15	495,000	230,500	46.57	0.81
Netherlands	14,400,000	14–17	103,267	46,368	44.90	0.65
Italy	58,000,000	12–18	375,100	239,000	63.72	0.65
Portugal	10,200,000	16–24	63,500	37,700	59.37	0.62
Denmark	5,150,000	9	31,400	9,500	30.25	0.61
Great Britain	56,000,000	Nil	325,909	Nil	Nil	0.58
Canada	25,000,000	Nil	82,858	Nil	Nil	0.33
Luxembourg	365,300	Nil	720	Nil	Nil	0.20
Iceland	240,000	Nil	Nil	Nil	Nil	0.00
Totals	633,701,300		5,325,396			0.84

WARSAW PACT ARMED FORCES

Country	Population	Conscription period (Months)	Armed Forces	Conscripts	Conscripts as % Armed Forces	Armed Forces as % total population
USSR	274,300,000	24–36	6,250,000	Only officers are accepted as volunteers		2.3
Bulgaria	9,000,000	24–36	147,300	94,000	63.82	1.64
Czechoslovakia	15,500,000	24–36	207,250	118,000	56.94	1.34
East Germany	16,860,000	18–36	172,000	94,500	54.94	1.02
Hungary	10,740,000	18–24	105,000	58,000	55.24	0.98
Poland	36,900,000	24–36	323,250	185,000	57.23	0.88
Romania	23,000,000	15–30	189,500	109,000	57.52	0.82
Totals	386,300,000	—	7,394,300	—	—	1.91

tanks and 13,000 aircraft. The naval forces are impressive and, in the case of the Soviet Union, modern. Throughout, levels of training, tactics and equipment are improving all the time.

Standing forces

NATO standing forces total over five million but this figure includes 800,000 French and Spanish troops who are not formally committed. Without them, approximately 2.6 million personnel are stationed in Europe. There are a further 400,000 pseudo-military personnel. In all, there exist 82 divisions and 180 brigades, not all committed to NATO, 25,000 main battle tanks and 11,200 combat aircraft.

Mobilization will be of crucial importance to both Alliances. But whereas both blocs maintain large numbers of trained reserves, the Warsaw Pact, because of its more formalized military structure and the greater intensity and length of its conscript training, would probably be able to exploit its reserves more speedily and efficiently. The United States and United Kingdom maintain highly professional part-time forces, but there would be major logistical problems in getting them to their battle stations, not only safely, but fresh and fit to fight. Reinforcement response tests carried out in the recent Exercise Lionheart showed that although troops from as far away as Texas could be in position on the West German border very speedily, it would take time to get them up to full effectiveness on the ground.

Thus NATO would not only be outnumbered at the commencement of any conflict, but the imbalance would immediately increase. To enable parity to be regained, NATO equipment and training which, at its best, is superior to that of the Warsaw Pact, would have to be exploited to the full in the early stages.

While NATO suffers from geographical splits, from long supply routes and a lack of territorial depth, the Warsaw Pact also has its own problems. Although geographically a single entity, the borders with China and the Indian continent are long and remote and will still require effective defense. The four Soviet fleets are spread far apart, with three of the four main harbors at risk from ice and liable to blockade. It is therefore likely that the Warsaw Pact would have the bulk of its fleets at sea prior to the commencement of hostilities.

Above: The regular military parades popular with the Soviets demonstrate the kind of reserves held within the USSR. Here T-72 MBTs assemble in the streets of Moscow.

Inset: Bought and operated by NATO, the Boeing E3-A Sentry Airborne Warning and Control System (AWACS) can look deep into Warsaw Pact airspace to give SACEUR and his airforce commanders the early warning and control capability required to defend NATO's frontiers.

Conventional Land Forces

Below: Who's watching who? A US Army patrol observes activity along the inner German border, while being the object of scrutiny of East German border guards in the observation tower.

The Opposing Armies

Warsaw Pact forces opposing NATO Allied Command Europe (ACE) outnumber it appreciably in every field except that of the support and transport helicopter. This imbalance increases with the arrival of reinforcements for there are some 167 active or reinforceable divisions, together with nine airborne or air assault divisions, immediately facing NATO. The value of the latter, however, is reduced by the fact that the Warsaw Pact has only sufficient aircraft available to move two divisions simultaneously. To counter this threat, NATO has 88 active and mobilizable divisions including three airborne/air mobile divisions, all of which could be made battle-effective very quickly. A further 12 US Army and two US Marine Corps divisions, a cavalry brigade and a Canadian brigade could be earmarked for Europe if required. Indeed, four of these divisions already have their heavy equipment pre-positioned in Europe, so enabling them to be battle-ready almost immediately. A NATO division is larger than its Warsaw Pact equivalent, but inferior in armor and artillery.

Recently the Soviets have greatly improved their logistics and communications and can now rely on well-trained and effective support. Their engineering equipment is modern, and their river and obstacle-crossing potential are second to none.

Comparing strategies

Despite the superiority in manpower and equipment enjoyed by the Warsaw Pact, it is NATO, rather surprisingly, that has always taken the initiative in strategic thinking. Whereas the Soviet Union does not necessarily envisage a future war as being nuclear, NATO, from the outset, exploited its nuclear arsenal to the full, relying upon the "trip-wire" theory to threaten massive nuclear retaliation against any Soviet incursion into its territory. The Soviets preferred to rely upon sheer numbers, steadfastly refusing to modernize their tactics until after the death of Stalin in 1953.

After Khrushchev took power and Marshal Grechko became Commander-in-Chief, Soviet technology so improved that the USSR felt capable of matching US nuclear might. Thus, in the early 1960s, priority was given to the creation of a viable strategic rocket force at the expense of conventional ground forces. At the same time, in the West the concept of "trip-wire" defense was losing credibility in favour of "flexible response" Accordingly, NATO would meet a threat with comparable conventional resources and only go nuclear in response to a similar attack or as a last resort. No sooner had the Warsaw Pact adopted a nuclear bias to counter NATO in that field than it found itself having to rethink its conventional operations policy.

Under the latest battle plan, the Warsaw Pact will attempt to snatch as much territory as it can in the opening period of any conflict, before NATO commanders gain permission to use nuclear weapons. The Soviets will attack in a single echelon, probably without waiting for full reinforcements, in the hope of reaching the Rhine during the initial pre-nuclear phase. Speed and surprise have therefore become the cornerstone of Soviet doctrine. In the words of Marshal Sokolovsky: "Not even the wealthiest of countries can afford to keep the whole of its armed forces deployed in peacetime. The only solution is to keep sufficient armed forces deployed in peacetime to reach, at least, the nearest strategic objectives (the Rhine) before successive echelons are mobilized and sent into action."

"Flexible response"

Whereas all NATO members supported in principle the introduction of the "flexible response" concept in 1967, there were, until recently, sharp policy divisions – particularly between West Germany and Britain – over whether an enemy offensive should be met on the border itself or be allowed first to cross the border, and then be disrupted and slowed by a covering force and ultimately destroyed in a series of preordained killing zones.

Geographically, NATO forces tend to be stationed in large pre-war barracks in areas where their predecessors were at the end of the war in 1945. It would be politically impossible today for these forces to be relocated and redeployed upon more acceptable military lines. Thus large quantities of US armor in the south face the mountains, while the vulnerable and flat Lüneberg Heath area of the north is guarded by far fewer and less well-equipped Dutch and Belgian troops.

The majority of West German troops are stationed not on the border, but deeper within the country so as to enable them to counter any Soviet incursion behind the front line. Quite naturally, by far the largest army serving in West Germany is the Bundeswehr, consisting of 495,000 men. Also stationed in West Germany are 233,000 US soldiers, 65,000 Britons, 50,000 French, 32,000 Belgians, 6,700 Dutch and 5,400 Canadians. There are also 3,700 Americans, 3,100 Britons and 2,700 Frenchmen based in West Berlin. These are formally a part of the Rhine armies but are nevertheless an integral part of NATO. However, no one would expect this small force to show more than token resistance in the face of overwhelming Soviet superiority and they might even be withdrawn prior to any conflict.

In principle, "flexible response" offers NATO a firm basis for the future, though it is very expensive in men and equipment and requires a firm commitment on behalf of all members – not just those with nuclear potential. The United States has often alleged that many of her allies are not pulling their weight, a view supported by Lord Home of the Hirsel, a former British Foreign Minister who, as long ago as October 1977, claimed: "the Allies have now reduced expenditure on conventional arms to a point where we are back to the policy of the 'trip-wire', that in response to any attack on Germany by the Soviet Union armies the tactical nuclear weapon would have to be used at once."

Top: NATO defense exercise in West Germany. Soldiers of the British Territorial Army armed with a machine gun and anti-tank gun counterattack through the streets of Rinteln. Behind them, life goes on as usual.

Right: Under the lee of a West German barn, two Leopard tanks move off, leaving behind a Transportpanzer 1, the armored personnel carrier currently in service with the West German army.

Top right: Warsaw Pact exercise. A combined force of Soviet T-54s, T-55s and BTR-60PBs approaches its objective. The infantry, having dismounted, move forward under cover of fire from the tanks.

Bottom right: A soldier of NATO's special forces. In time of war, they would have to operate behind enemy lines, gathering intelligence, seeking out targets and guiding weapon systems onto them. This is a lonely, risky job requiring the highest degree of training.

The Soldier

No matter how technologically advanced a modern army may be, unless the soldier in the field is sufficiently motivated and trained to use his equipment to the full, much of that army's potential will be lost.

NATO

With the exception of the USA and UK, NATO forces rely heavily on conscription, and so for most young soldiers their period of national service is one of necessity rather than enjoyment.

The United States relied upon conscription for many years but its military presence in Vietnam became so unpopular with the nation's youth that the draft was scrapped. The army is now manned exclusively by volunteers and many Europeans feel that the United States made too many compromises in building up its volunteer forces quickly, and that discipline has suffered as a result.

The UK has always disliked conscription, preferring to rely upon a small but highly-trained and motivated professional army. This is an expensive option, and the difficulty in maintaining pay scales and other constraints on expenditure (such as the constant shortage of training material) has considerably sapped morale at times.

Although his enthusiasm for peacetime soldiering may not be

A potent specialist force available for intervention in trouble spots worldwide, American paratroopers storm off a drop zone, giving each other covering fire. Around them, reinforcements continue to arrive, dropped by Hercules transport aircraft.

great, there is no reason to believe that the European conscript would not defend his homeland to the best of his ability in time of war.

The Soviet Union

In contrast to this, the Soviet citizen and, to a lesser extent, his Warsaw Pact counterpart, is introduced to military service far earlier. Both boys and girls receive practical training in the rudiments of military discipline, regulations, drill, guard duty and civil defense. At the age of 15 the schoolchild may join the Komsomol (Young Communist League for 15- to 28-year-olds) and will attend Orlyonok ("Young Eagle") camps to extend his knowledge of map-reading, weapons and grenade-throwing.

Unless there are serious medical or domestic problems, or he has yet to finish his education – in which case enrolment will be deferred – the young Soviet citizen will be drafted straight after his 18th birthday. Conscription is usually for two years in the army, or three years in the navy or strategic rocket force. Conscripts are called up en masse every six months, with the result that a highly undesirable four-tier society has evolved within the barrack block. The conscript earns 3–5 roubles (about $10) per month, is not allowed to wear civilian clothes, receives no leave for the entire period of his duty and is confined to barracks for the majority of his service. Alcohol is banned from barracks. Discipline is harsh and physical and often enforced on the basis of "collective responsibility". An entire squad is punished for the offence of one of its members, with the intention that the squad will ensure, privately, that the individual behaves himself in the future. Capital punishment is still suffered by deserters at all times and is meted out for several offenses.

Training is highly structured and intensively physical. Several

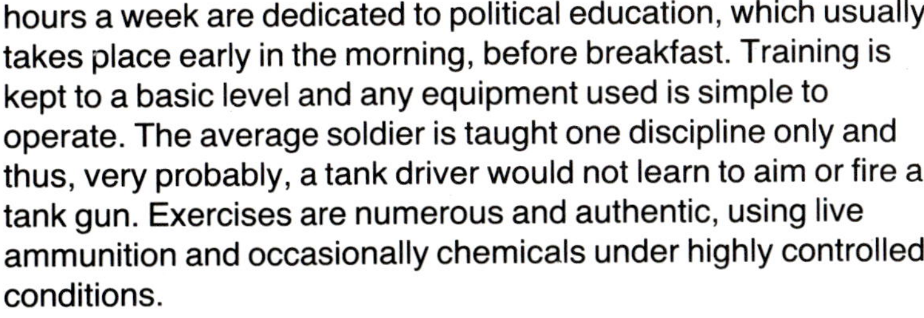

hours a week are dedicated to political education, which usually takes place early in the morning, before breakfast. Training is kept to a basic level and any equipment used is simple to operate. The average soldier is taught one discipline only and thus, very probably, a tank driver would not learn to aim or fire a tank gun. Exercises are numerous and authentic, using live ammunition and occasionally chemicals under highly controlled conditions.

Top: Dutch conscripts during their 14–16 months in the army train on the American developed TOW missile – one of the most numerous of ATGW systems in service with the majority of NATO armies.

Right: Soldiers in the making. Recruits for the reserve army march along a road at Fort Campbell, Kentucky, singing as they go. It's all part of the process of converting civilians into efficient, fit and disciplined servicemen.

Junior NCOs are often chosen before they begin their service and are sent on highly exacting six-month service courses before being allocated to a unit. Their role is to carry out orders and under no circumstances to use their initiative. Senior NCOs are all volunteers who have accepted an invitation to remain in the armed forces after conscription. Pay and conditions improve immediately – so much so that the average senior NCO will command a standard of living comfortably above that of many civilians.

Officers attend a four-year course at one of several academies, each specializing in one field of military training. Whereas an officer cadet at West Point Academy or the Royal Military Academy at Sandhurst will have the opportunity to see much of service life before choosing his specialization, his Soviet equivalent will be denied this opportunity. The life of a junior officer is rigidly structured and constantly under the eye of the Political Officer who can veto the promotion of any officer unwise enough to voice unorthodox opinions.

Whatever may be lacking in the Soviet military system, it nevertheless works. Few countries in the world rely so heavily upon the sheer unabated patriotism of its people as does the Soviet Union. If the Soviet soldier can be convinced to fight for his Fatherland, and that any failure on his part will lead to a repeat of the carnage of the Great Patriotic War, he will fight as bravely and tenaciously as his forefathers have done from the time of Peter the Great.

Top center: Encouraged by his instructor, a US reserve trainee tries to clear his body of tear gas after a visit to a gas chamber – a necessary preparation for the possible use of chemical weapons during a future conflict.

Top right: With many regions of the USSR remote and mountainous, and part of Europe inaccessible to armored units, the Soviet mountain troops have an important role in defense and in operations abroad, such as Afghanistan.

Bottom right: A Soviet forward command and observation post. Leaving most of their staff in headquarters to the rear, a Soviet battalion commander may set up such a post to retain mobility and flexibility during an advance.

Below: Red alert. Soviet signallers led by a sergeant, double to their posts past their colleague on sentry duty.

THE SOVIET SOLDIER'S DAILY ROUTINE (Voiennyi Vestnik, January 1976)

	Activity	Time	Time taken
1.	Reveille	0600–0605	5 mins
2.	Physical training (and room cleaning)	0610–0630	20 mins
3.	Wash (and make beds)	0630–0650	20 mins
4.	Political information class (morning summary)	0650–0720	30 mins
5.	Breakfast	0725–0755	30 mins
6.	1st hour of lessons 6th hour of lessons	0800–0850 1300–1350	50 mins 50 mins
7.	Lunch	1400–1440	40 mins
8.	After-lunch break	1440–1510	30 mins
9.	Maintenance of personal weapon and equipment	1510–1530	20 mins
10a. b. c.	Political education lesson (Monday and Thursday) Technical maintenance (Tuesday and Friday) Sport (Wednesday and Saturday)	1530–1830	3 hours
11.	Self tuition	1830–1940	1 hour 10 mins
12.	Supper	1940–2010	30 mins
13.	Free time	2010–2140	1 hour 30 mins
14.	Evening walk and roll-call	2140–2155	15 mins
15.	Lights out	2200	

Main Battle Tanks

The Warsaw Pact

Soviet tanks have always been built to a cheap, rugged design, encompassing good firepower, mobility and armored protection. Easy to maintain, they have required little support and only a minimum of crew training. With the introduction of the T-64, with its automatic loader and three-man crew, this advantage is now diminishing. Although the low silhouette common to all Soviet tanks is a good basic protection against antitank fire, crew comfort is sacrificed as a direct result. Therefore it is often the crew, rather than the vehicle, who show the first signs of fatigue on exercise.

The Soviet T54/55

Even with the introduction of such modern technology as the laser rangefinder fitted to the latest T-72s, a Soviet tank costs little more than one third of its American equivalent – with the result that financial restrictions have never limited production. Between 1949 and 1979, when production finally ceased, over 45,000 T54/55 tanks were constructed at the Nizhnii Tagil Works. Of these, approximately 20,000 were exported to allies throughout the Warsaw Pact, Middle East and Africa and the rest retained within the Soviet Army. Despite its age, the T54/55 remains a very able weapon and still forms the backbone of most Soviet rear echelon divisions. Armed with a D-10T 100-mm-rifled tank-gun, rounds of high-explosive, antitank (HEAT) fragmentation can be fired over an effective range of 1,250 yards (1,125m). The basic load of 43 rounds is small by NATO standards, the problem emphasized by the lack of ready-use ammunition caused by the extreme lack of crew space. The 580 hp V-12 water-cooled diesel engine can achieve a top road speed of 31.5 mph (50 km/h) and, most important in the Soviet winter, does not suffer in the extreme cold. Although the T54/55 will not be found in GSFG (Ground Soviet Forces Germany) it is still the

Above: T-72 is the latest Soviet MBT for which information is available. It has a 125-mm gun and modern laminate armor and is significantly lighter and lower than its NATO counterparts.

Left: A commander and gunner study the route as a company of American M60A3s, one with a full width dozer blade, wait for fresh orders. The M60A3 is an upgraded version of A1, comparable to the Soviet T-72.

mainstay of several Warsaw Pact Forces and, rather strangely, is still being built under license in China.

The T-62

The subsequent T-62, first built at Kharkov in 1961, was only of limited success and when production finally ceased in the early 1970s only some 13,000 had been built, of which approximately 6,000 were distributed among the Warsaw Pact. The higher cost of the T-62 (almost five times that of the T-55) discouraged non-Warsaw Pact countries from purchasing it, with the result that the Soviet Union was left with approximately 7,000 models out of necessity, rather than choice. Armed with a 115-mm USTS tank gun and 12.7-mm antiaircraft machine gun, the T-62 has an extremely low rate of fire, made worse by its inability to fire on the move. Furthermore the automatic recoil system, which ejects spent rounds through a hole in the rear of the turret, often fails to work – so that shells are discarded among crew, often with dire results. When the system does work, it reduces the crew's NBC (nuclear/biological/chemical) protection level to the extent that they have to operate in hot and cumbersome rubber suits.

The T-62 saw battle service against Israeli M-40s, M-60s and Centurions and proved to be no match. Considering that this tank forms the offensive spearhead of most of today's non-Soviet Warsaw Pact armored divisions, it is easy to realize that many of these divisions would suffer badly in any conflict with NATO armor.

The T-64

When the T-64 was first seen in GSFG in 1970, its design was so different to its predecessors that it took the West completely by surprise. In order to accommodate the large new 125-mm gun without increasing the interior dimensions, an automatic loader has replaced the gunner, but it is understood that this system is still giving problems some fifteen years later. The new Rapira

WARSAW PACT MAIN BATTLE TANKS

Type	Crew	Weight	Height	Speed	Main Armament	Range	Vehicle Range
		lbs/kg	ft/m	mph/km/h	mm	yds/m	miles/km
T-72	3	91,000/41,000	7.5/2.25	50/80	125	2,250/2,050	280/450
T-64	3	77,000/35,000	7.5/2.25	43/69	125	2,250/2,050	280/450
T-62	4	82,000/37,000	7.9/2.4	28/45	115	1,800/1,600	280/450
T-54/55	4	79,000/36,000	7.9/2.4	30/48	100	1,250/1,150	310/500

A column of Soviet T-62s of a guards tank regiment drive through the summer dust, displaying their 115-mm smooth-bore gun. Developed from the T-54/55, the T-62 was outgunned by the Israeli 105-mm rifled guns during the Middle East wars.

125-mm main gun can fire up to 8 rounds per minute, is stabilized and can penetrate all NATO armor. With the day sight the gun has a range of 2,250 yards (2,025 m); with the night sight, 900 yards (810 m). A mixture of ceramic and rolled steel armor has been used on the front of the chassis to enhance protection from all but the largest antitank missiles. However, several T-72s constructed with the same armor were destroyed by the Israelis in 1982 and its exact worth must therefore remain questionable.

Due to a combination of expense and technical problems, the T-64 was never exported. There is some dispute as to how many were actually built, the number varying between 3,000 and 6,000, but what is certain is that T-64 divisions form a large part of 3 Shock Army within GSFG and will play an important part in any hostilities for years to come.

The T-72

The Soviets regarded the T-64 in many ways as a prototype and began developing a new tank soon after the ordering of T-64 production. The resultant T-72 incorporates most of the innovations found in the T-64, together with new wheels, tracks, suspension and a larger 780 hp V-12 diesel engine. Capable of a maximum road speed of 38 mph (61 km/h) the T-72 has excellent cross-country capability, is fitted with a snorkel enabling it to wade to a depth of nearly 18 feet (5.4 m) and is fully pressurized – allowing the crew to operate in contaminated conditions without protective suits.

Over 10,000 T-72s have now been built, many under license at Katowice in Poland and Pilsen in Czechoslovakia, and several variants exist. Indeed many tanks now being described erroneously as T-80 are in fact T-72 variants. The Soviets have exported models of this tank to Libya and Syria but they lack many of the internal systems, such as the fire control system and laser rangefinder incorporated in Soviet models. It is therefore wrong to assume that NATO would find it as easy to defeat a

Left: With a 100-mm main gun the T-55 was the mainstay of the Warsaw Pact armored units until it was replaced by the T-62. Though now obsolete, it is still found in the rear areas and remains, along with the T-62, the most common tank in the army.

Below: Used by Soviet naval infantry, and fully amphibious, the PT-76 light tank is armed with a 76.2-mm gun. The PT-76 is a large tank but has had to sacrifice armor protection for the sake of being amphibious.

Soviet T-72M as did the Israelis in defeating the basic Syrian models. The T-72 on the whole is a very competitive tank. It is still a good match for the M-60 and Leopard I and, although inferior to later NATO tanks, it has the advantage of sheer numbers. The Soviets are well aware of the problems inherent in the T-72, particularly crew fatigue and the automatic loader – and it is highly likely that a revolutionary new Soviet tank will appear within the next few years.

Above: A Leopard 1A3, belonging to the Canadian brigade group based in Germany, sports an improvised camouflage scheme for the snowy weather. Its 105-mm L7 gun can fire all standard NATO ammunition.

Below: Arguably the best MBT on the battlefield today, the Leopard 2 has a 120-mm smoothbore gun and Chobham-type armor. In recent tank competitions it was superior to both the US Abrams and the British Challenger.

NATO

NATO has always accepted that its MBTs will be heavily outnumbered in any central European conflict and consequently has relied on a combination of superior armor, firepower, ammunition and training to combat this. Despite the obvious advantages, the main tank producers, Britain, France, West Germany and the United States, have failed totally to agree to any form of standardization. Millions of scarce dollars are consequently being spent on duplicated research, development and production.

West Germany

When West Germany rebuilt its army in 1955, it was equipped with old American M-47s and M-48s, with some M-48s retained for training purposes. France, Italy and West Germany all required a new MBT and it was agreed that France and West Germany would each produce a prototype for independent evaluation, the winner to be jointly produced thereafter. National rivalries proved too powerful, however; France produced the AMX-30 while West Germany's Leopard went into production.

The Leopard 1 and 2

After three years of development, production of the Leopard began in 1963 at the Krauss-Maffei Works in Munich; the first model was accepted by the Bundeswehr on September 9 1965. Incorporating an MTU MB 838 10-cylinder multifuel engine capable of developing 830 hp, the Leopard I was capable of reaching a road speed of 40 mph (64 km/h) over a range of 348

Above: The M-60, with its 105-mm L7 series gun of British design, will continue to be an important part of the US inventory for a long time yet, though the M1 Abrams is now entering service in numbers.

Left: Compared with the other tanks in NATO, France's AMX-30 is poorly armored and would find it difficult to take on the latest Soviet tanks.

miles (557 km). The turret was German, built by Rheinmetall and Wegmann, and the incorporated gun was the tried and tested British L7 105-mm tank-gun, then regarded as the world's finest.

Subsequent models of the Leopard included a stabilizing system enabling the tank to fire on the move (Leopard I A1), and a new wedge-shaped turret of spaced armor to allow for greater stowage space (Leopard I A3). The incorporation of a reliable engine, lacking in the British Centurion, and a powerful main gun, lacking in the American M-48, gave the Leopard excellent export potential. It is now the principal tank in service with Australia, Belgium, Canada, Denmark, Italy, the Netherlands and Norway, as well as with the rear echelons of the Bundeswehr itself.

The Leopard I was a match for any tank of its day, but NATO realized the necessity for greater armored protection and firepower – and so development of the Leopard 2 began in the late 1960s. The West Germans and the United States had agreed jointly to develop the MBT-70, and when the latter cancelled this agreement in January 1970, the project was given a much higher priority in Germany. The resultant Leopard 2 is arguably the finest MBT presently in operational service anywhere in the world. The new MTU 873 Ka-500 multifuel engine gives the vehicle a maximum road speed of 42 mph (67 km/h) over a range of 342 miles (547 km). The hull and turret are of all-welded construction, while the hull front and turret have the added protection of spaced armor. The completely new Rheinmetall 120-mm smoothbore gun, with its drop-type breech and hydraulically-assisted loading mechanism, can fire fin-stabilized APDS (armor-piercing discarding sabot) and multi-purpose rounds to an effective distance of 3,300 yards (2,970 m). The interior is fully NBC-proofed.

Bottom: A Rhine barge packed with M-60 MBTs and armored recovery vehicles belonging to US-based reinforcements enters a river lock. The strategic potential of the European waterways is considerable.

Right: Currently equipping armored units of the US Army in Germany, the M1 Abrams, if it lives up to expectations, has the potential to be a formidable battlefield weapon capable of taking on any opponent.

France

Originally, France started development of a new MBT with West Germany, but when it was found that fundamental design disagreements could not be overcome, each country continued development independently and the AMX-30 resulted. The prototype was completed in 1960, with production following at Satory, near Versailles, from 1963. For political reasons, the

French shunned the British L7 tank gun, preferring to develop their own 105-mm quick-fire semiautomatic weapon. The French gun lacks stabilization, with the result that it cannot fire on the move. Its ammunition is also specialized and cannot be interchanged with that of any other NATO tank. Resupply problems would most likely abound in time of war. Although the AMX-30 is extremely agile, it is far too lightly-armored to engage modern Soviet tanks head-on, and would have to rely upon its maneuverability to survive.

The French army is presently being re-equipped with the AMX-30B2, featuring improved transmission, fire control and fin-stabilized ammunition as a stop-gap. However, France will not be able to play a full part in a European tank battle until the introduction of the radically new AMX-40 in the 1990s, with its redesigned chassis, engine and 120-mm gun.

United States

Development of US tanks has, until recently, been piecemeal. The M-47 was not a success and, although it was exported or donated to friendly governments around the world, it was never fully adopted by the USA itself. The M-48, first produced in 1952, was heavier and more successful – but its original 90-mm gun, fitted to all but the latest M-48-A5 model, is now considered woefully inadequate. Turkey, the only NATO member still to use the M-48 as a front-line MBT, is presently utilizing a US grant to re-engine aging tanks and to re-equip them with the far superior British L7 gun. West Germany and the United States still keep fleets of M-48s, but only for training and reserve purposes.

Still the basic tank of the US armed forces, the M-60 series started production in 1959 and continued at the Detroit Tank

Arsenal for the next 25 years. Equipped originally with the AVDS-1790-2 engine and British L7 gun, built under license in the United States, the M-60 was capable of road speeds of 30 mph (48 km/h) over a distance of 342 miles (547 km). Production of the M-60 proceeded smoothly, with over 3,000 models leaving the production line in the first fifteen years. However, development was hindered by government insistence that priority be given to the fitting of a turret capable of mounting the Shillelagh rocket system. The resultant M60-A2 proved to be a disaster and except for a few trialled in West Germany, all have now been withdrawn from service. The M-60 is no real match for the latest Warsaw Pact MBTs due to its great height, slow speed and old gun. But the M-60 still comprises over 70 per cent of United States armored strength within NATO.

The M-1 Abrams

The necessity for a new MBT led to contracts being awarded to Chrysler Corporation and General Motors each to produce a revolutionary new prototype. In 1976 it was announced that the Chrysler Corporation's design, subsequently designated the M-1 Abrams, would be put into production. Superficially years ahead of its time, the Abrams incorporates a considerable amount of European technology. The hull and turret are constructed of new British Chobham armor, making it immune from attack from all but the heaviest missiles. Armament consisted originally of the British L7 gun, manufactured under license in the United States, but this is now being replaced with the new German Rheinmetall 120-mm smooth-bore gun. Both guns are stabilized and supported by an advanced laser target location system. A full NBC system is fitted whilst ammunition and fuel supplies are segregated from the crew by metal bulkheads for added safety. Unfortunately the highly-powered gas turbine engine, which allows acceleration from 0 to 20 mph (32 km/h) in six seconds, is very noisy and overheats easily. The Abrams will not be able to take its full place in the NATO arsenal until this fundamental problem is resolved.

Britain

Since the introduction of the Centurion Mk I in 1945, Britain has led the world in tank gun technology and defensive armor. But British tank engines have always been underpowered and

The most successful of British tanks since World War II has been the Centurion Mk 5/2. Now nearing the end of its effective life, the Centurion still serves with the Danish Army, along with the Leopard 1. Like the Leopard, it has a 105-mm L7 gun.

Top left: M-1 Abrams seen firing its 105-mm main armament against a night sky. With the latest armor, the M1 Abrams presents a substantial improvement over the M60 it replaces.

Bottom left: The AMX-40 is a marked improvement on the earlier AMX-30. It has laminated armor and, like the Leopard 2 and Abrams, a 120-mm smoothbore gun capable of firing standard ammunition.

Bottom right: Chieftains exercising in West Germany. The Chieftain, despite the introduction of the Challenger, can be expected to equip front-line armored regiments until the turn of the century.

NATO MAIN BATTLE TANKS

Type	Crew	Weight lbs/kg	Height ft/m	Speed mph/km/h	Main Armament mm	Range yds/m	Vehicle Range miles/km
AMX 30	4	82,000/37,000	9.3/2.8	40/64	105	2,250/2,050	400/640
Centurion	4	114,000/51,000	9.8/2.9	22/35	105	2,250/2,050	120/190
Chieftain	4	121,000/54,000	9.5/2.85	30/48	120	3,300+/3,000+	310/500
Challenger	4	132,000/59,000	9.5/2.85	35/56	120	3,300+/3,000+	310/500
Leopard 1	4	89,000/40,000	8.6/2.6	40/64	105	2,250/2,050	350/550
Leopard 2	4	125,000/56,000	8.00/2.4	42/67	120	3,300+/3,000+	340/540
M-60	4	115,000/52,000	10.7/3.2	30/48	105	2,250/2,050	340/540
Abrams	4	120,000/54,000	7.8/2.3	45/72	105	2,250/2,050	270/430

therefore vulnerable. Over 4,000 Centurions were produced, of which 2,500 were exported, and indeed the Mk 13 is still in NATO service with Denmark.

Although numerous attempts were made during the early 1950s to develop a replacement, the Chieftain was not accepted into service until 1963. Equipped with the L11A5 120-mm rifled tank gun and supported by the latest target acquisition equipment, the Chieftain is powered by a Leyland L60 12-cylinder multifuel engine but is capable of no more than 30 mph (48 km/h) on the open road. Breakdowns are common. The British government is now replacing Chieftain with Challenger, with its superb Chobham armor, proven 120-mm gun and much improved engine – but financial constraints are such that Chieftain will remain Britain's principal MBT for many years to come.

Armored Personnel Carriers

Warsaw Pact

In order to win a speedy war before its losses become too great or before the catastrophe of nuclear escalation, the Soviet Union must maintain the ability to transport its infantry as fast as its armor. During the advances through Poland in 1944 and into Germany in 1945, infantry sections clung precariously to the chassis of the advancing T-34s in the hope that this would at least afford them some protection against mines. Inevitably, their losses from shrapnel and small arms were tremendous.

According to Soviet military doctrine, it is necessary for the infantry to close with and destroy the enemy with as little delay as possible. To execute such a move, not only must the infantry be carried virtually to the enemy's front line but it must be given withering small arms protection thereafter. So, it is not surprising that Soviet, and hence Warsaw Pact, personnel carriers have not only been armored and mobile since their inception, but also heavily armed.

Early Soviet efforts to build armored personnel carriers (APCs) were compromised by a lack of money and the latest technology. Whereas the West started to develop tracked vehicles immediately after World War II, the Soviets had to content themselves with wheeled vehicles. This problem has never been fully overcome and even today the majority of infantry supporting Motor-Rifle Divisions will travel in wheeled APCs.

Top left: An unusual interior view of a BTR-60, with the driver's seat at left and the commander's at right. Compared with its complex NATO counterparts the BTR-60 is spartan and basic.

Far left: Challenger has a similar gun to Chieftain, but with its Chobham armor, hydrogas suspension and much more powerful engine, Challenger offers the British Royal Armoured Corps a much improved tank.

Top: Infantry will normally dismount from their APCs as they approach an objective to fight through on foot. Here they are being given covering fire from BMP-1s, with the nearest two carrying Sagger ATGWs.

Left: Even the highly successful NATO M113 APC requires repairs occasionally. Here an M113 engine from a M577 Command Post is being worked on, with a M88 Medium ARV in the background.

The BTR-60 Series

Although a few old BTR-152s remain in service with East Germany and may be found occasionally acting as command posts, the majority of wheeled APCs presently in service with the Warsaw Pact belong to the BTR-60 series. Easy to operate and maintain, cheap to build and amphibious, the first BTR-60s to enter service were open-topped. This obvious shortfall was soon rectified with the advent of the roofed BTR-60PA, which is still to be found with many units in the role of communications vehicle. The BTR-60PB, with its armored turret mounting a 14.5-mm machine-gun, first entered service in 1965 and is at present the standard wheeled APC of the Warsaw Pact. Served by a crew of three (driver, gunner, commander), it can carry up to nine fully-equipped passengers. The latter can utilize the three firing-ports on either side of the hull to fire their personal weapons while the vehicle goes into action, but in so doing they will certainly compromise their NBC protection.

If the BTR-60PB's advantage lies in its firepower – and many vehicles are now equipped with an AGS-17 capable of firing 30-mm grenades up to distances in excess of 1,000 yards (900 m) – this is outweighed by several disadvantages. Equipped with an unnecessarily complicated system of twin engines, the vehicle is nevertheless so underpowered that it has difficulty in surmounting rough terrain and in making river crossings, if the far river bank is steep or muddy. Its armor is so thin that it offers no protection against 7.62-mm armor-piercing rounds; the petrol engines require large tanks of highly inflammable fuel and the infantry are forced to exit from two highly vulnerable hatches on the vehicle top. Moreover the wheel base is so wide that it cannot be used in conjunction with the majority of Warsaw Pact mine-clearing equipment. If a BTR-60PB unit were proceeding against a well-defended, mined position, the infantry would have to debus on their own side of the minefield, possibly whilst under enemy fire – and would then have to bunch through the minefield along the tracks made by the supporting tanks. A terrible prospect for any infantryman!

Late in 1978 the Soviets introduced a larger and more advanced APC, designated BTR-70PB, but this has not proved a success. Equipped with a larger engine and small hatches either side of the chassis to offer the infantry more protection when dismounting, the design was outdated at its inception – and although built under license in East Germany for a short time, few of this model will be seen in service with the Warsaw Pact armies.

The Soviet BMP

Since the 1960s, the Warsaw Pact has been aware of the necessity for a reliable, well-armored tracked vehicle capable both of supporting its tanks and carrying the infantry deep into an enemy position. The BMP (*Boyevaya Mashina Pekhoty*), which entered service in 1967, met these requirements adequately and was, without doubt, the most advanced infantry fighting vehicle of its day. Capable of carrying a full section of eight men in the rear along with its crew of three, it is armed with

Left: Saxon wheeled APCs crossing a medium girder bridge. Of British design, this is one of the most successful and popular types of modern tactical bridging in service with NATO. It can carry a tank across gaps of 33 yards (30 m), or more using piers or pontoons.

Below: A British Saxon APC passing a Blowpipe post in Germany. Based on standard truck engineering, the Saxon is armed with a 762-mm GPMG; a cheap APC of limited capability, it is currently equipping units in BAOR and Britain.

a 73-mm gun capable of engaging armor at 1,400 yards (1,250 m) and the Sagger antitank wire-guided missile with a range in excess of 2,500 yards (2,250 m). In true Soviet tradition, the vehicle is fitted with firing ports to enable the infantry to engage the enemy up to the very second of debussing. Although the BMP is classed as an amphibious vehicle, it reacts awkwardly in water and can only attain a speed of 5 mph (8 km/h). Two large doors are fitted to the rear to enable the infantry to dismount with a degree of safety, but the crew still has to dismount through hatches in the top.

The BMP, though advanced for its day, suffers from several drawbacks. The armor protection is thin (19 mm in the hull and 23 mm in the turret), and is only resistant to heavy machine-gun fire over the frontal arc. It has a very high vibration problem at top speed and transmission problems at 45 mph (72 km/h). The land navigation system must be re-zeroed every 30 minutes, the passenger quarters are extremely cramped and uncomfortable and the Sagger, which must be reloaded externally, can only be fired from a stationary position. Most fatal of all, extra fuel is stored in tanks built into the rear doors. These are not well protected and a 0.5-inch incendiary round fired into the rear doors will cause these to explode with catastrophic consequences for the passengers.

With the advent of much-improved NATO APCs in the late 1970s came the realization within the Warsaw Pact that it would need to re-equip itself or be totally outgunned. Rather than waste time and money on totally new development, the Soviets merely designed a new turret for the existing BMP chassis. The new vehicle, designated BMP-2, has a much larger two-man turret, containing a new 30-mm cannon. Smoke-grenade launchers and an infrared searchlight are also fitted, while the old Sagger is replaced by the more accurate AT-5, Spandrel.

The BMP-2 has the capacity of destroying virtually all NATO armor and must be regarded as one of the most formidable APCs in existence; presently only in service with front-line Soviet divisions, the BMP-2 will certainly be introduced throughout the Warsaw Pact as soon as supply permits.

NATO

The US M113

Without doubt the most successful APC of all time must be the United States M113, designed in the late 1950s. Over 40,000 have been produced; around 32,000 are presently in NATO service. Its aluminum construction makes the vehicle extremely light with good amphibious qualities. However, aluminum provides poor protection against mines. Despite the M113's all-round excellence, it is too lightly armored and is armed only for an independent offensive role. The British FV432 is of similar design, but being of steel construction, is considerably heavier. Both vehicles have adapted well to such versatile roles as ambulance, maintenance, command and antitank missile launchers – but both have severely hampered the tactical advances of their user nations due to their vulnerability.

The German Marder MICV

West Germany insisted from the outset that it would not yield sovereign territory in time of war, and was the first NATO member to design an APC capable of engaging a massed enemy formation. The German Marder MICV first entered service in 1971 and is large enough to contain a crew of 10 (commander, driver, two gunners and six infantrymen). Armed with a 20-mm cannon and 7.62-mm coaxial machine-gun in its forward turret, the Marder has a unique sting in the tail provided by a remotely-controlled 7.62-mm machine-gun mounted at the rear of the hull. At 31.5 tons, the vehicle is far too heavy to have any form of amphibious capability, but this is not considered important when weighed against the benefits of added protection afforded by the heavier armor. Marder was the first NATO troop carrier to incorporate firing ports in the hull – enabling the infantry to engage a target without dismounting.

During the last decade both Great Britain and the United States have come to appreciate the Marder concept and each nation has recently developed its own heavy, well-armed troop carrier.

The M-2 Bradley

The United States M-2 Bradley has the appearance of a small tank. Over three feet (about one meter) taller than the Soviet BMP, the height disadvantage is more than compensated for by the vehicle providing a considerably more comfortable ride. Out of an intended 6,800 vehicles, over 2,000 had been delivered by the end of 1985; on the basis of present production the entire US army in Germany should be equipped with the Bradley by the end of 1986.

The M-2 Bradley incorporates the German concept of sealed ports to enable the infantry to fire from within the vehicle. The main armament consists of a 25-mm chain gun that fires a tungsten penetrator capable of defeating the frontal armor of all Soviet APCs at ranges up to 1,100 yards (990 m) and a Belgian-designed MAG-58 7.62-mm machine-gun for local protection. It is significant that twin TOW ATGMs have been fitted for the first time. Seven missiles are carried (the BMP carries only four) and reloading is possible from within the protected fighting compartment.

Similar to the M-2 is the M-3 Cavalry Fighting Vehicle built for screening, reconnaissance and security roles. To equip armored cavalry units and scout platoons of mechanized infantry and tank battalions, it carries a crew of five, with additional 25-mm ammunition and 10 TOW missiles. The firing ports are not used.

It was Britain's original intention to purchase the American M-2 Bradley, but for economic reasons subsequently decided to

Left: With the arrival of Warrior (MCV-80) and Challenger, the British Army is being re-equipped to an unprecedented high standard. But high equipment costs and budget constraints are likely to limit their distribution and ultimate effectiveness.

Below: A versatile, well-designed vehicle, the Renault VAB APC is equipped with a turret mounting four HOT antitank missiles. It is now entering service with the French Army.

develop its own personnel carrier and awarded the contract to GKN Sankey. The resultant vehicle, orginally designated the MCV-80 but now officially named "Warrior", is even heavier than the M-2 Bradley. Capable of transporting seven fully equipped troops plus the driver, commander and gunner, the Warrior, with its all-welded aluminum-armored hull affords protection against small arms fire and shell burst fragments. The two-man steel turret contains a 30-mm Rarden cannon capable of immobilizing enemy APCs and a coaxial 7.62-mm chain gun to give protection to advancing infantry, once dismounted.

Wheeled APCs will continue to see service throughout NATO as a far cheaper option, as many roles do not require the mobility, firepower and protection of the tracked MICV. France, for instance, is introducing the twelve-seater Renault VAB APC; Britain has selected the Saxon as its "battlefield taxi", and Germany will continue to use the Transportpanzer 1 Multi-Purpose Armored Vehicle for some time to come.

Personnel carriers such as Marder, Bradley and Warrior are a more than adequate match for their Warsaw Pact equivalents and are capable of fighting alongside their MBTs. However, they all lack two Soviet advantages: simplicity and cheapness. In the future, financially-conscious NATO may find it necessary to return to smaller, simpler vehicles in order to achieve quantity as well as quality.

Reconnaissance

Warsaw Pact

According to Warsaw Pact doctrine, timely and comprehensive reconnaissance (or "recce" for short) is the key to success. It is carried out on a large scale, using a wide variety of assets, and is intensive and continuous. Unlike NATO, the Warsaw Pact

Far left: Marder is the state-of-the-art MICV, with good protection mobility and armament – here seen with its driver taking a break. Note the 20-mm cannon and the mount for the remote-controlled 7.62-mm MG at the rear of the hull.

Left: This British Scimitar, with its 30-mm Rarden cannon, has successfully "killed" a Bundswehr Leopard 1 while on exercise in Germany, showing how the lightly armed recce vehicle can be used to its full effect.

Bottom: Three Soviet BRDM-2s on nighttime patrol. These versatile recce vehicles can carry a crew of four, are armed with turret-mounted 14.5-mm and coaxial 7.62-mm machine guns, and can be used as a missile platform for ATGWs or SAMs.

employs extensive multiple ground patrols on all sides of its operations. A divisional commander can call upon up to three layers of patrols ahead of him, together with a wide variety of air and engineering recce.

Technologically a recce patrol is a combination of old and new equipment. The BRDM-2, which is found in all patrols, is an amphibious vehicle, armed with 14.5-mm and 7.62-mm machine-guns. Capable of operating under most conditions, it features a unique system of supplementary wheels under the chassis. These can be retracted when not required, but they cannot be halted when in motion and can cause an uncomfortable ride for the five passengers. A number of BMP variants have appeared in the last five years and are giving the Warsaw Pact a newly-found versatility, particularly in the area of communications.

Chemical/radiological reconnaissance is conducted at both divisional and regimental level by specially trained and equipped troops who have no equivalent within NATO. Using either the BRDM rkh or the MTLB rkh, these troops will advance into contaminated areas, marking the boundaries with flags fired mechanically from the rear of the vehicle.

Each artillery battery now boasts its own reconnaissance vehicle, an ACRV-2. It is equipped with laser rangefinder and passive night-vision devices. However, it is too lightly armored to withstand more than small arms fire and will not usually venture further forward than the front line.

Far left: Soviet officers pause for orders in front of BMP-1s. The 73-mm low pressure gun and Sagger antitank guided weapon (ATGW) are clearly visible on the lead vehicle – as a mechanical infantry combat vehicle (MICV) it proved vulnerable during the 1973 Arab/Israeli conflict.

Left: Drivers of a motor cycle and BRDM-2 in a Soviet recce patrol consult. Working well forward of their own troops, they could be tasked with locating and identifying enemy positions and would usually be supported by BMPs.

Below: Here seen launching a TOW 2 antitank missile, this US Army Bradley in its M3 Cavalry Fighting Vehicle variant will be able to take on any MBT with its TOW, and other armored vehicles with its 25-mm chain gun.

Warsaw Pact recce is well-trained, well-equipped and exploited to the full. Geared totally for a rapid advance, it anticipates heavy casualties but regards this as acceptable. Its main weakness lies in its lack of adaptability, and if it can be destroyed in the early stages of a battle, the leading divisions would find themselves blind and under considerable pressure.

NATO

NATO is well aware of its vulnerability behind the front line. In time of war, it is highly likely that the Warsaw Pact would utilize large numbers of airborne troops, the Soviet Union alone having eight divisions available, to attack key points in the rear. To link up with these forces, Operational Maneuver Groups would smash their way through weak points in the NATO defenses, thus completely destroying NATO lines of communications and supply. Over the past decade NATO has therefore developed a class of vehicle, capable not only of fulfilling the conventional reconnaissance role ahead of the main force, but also able to move at great speed against an enemy suddenly appearing to the rear.

Wheeled vehicles have the capability of long range and high speed when used on good road surfaces, offering an ideal mobile response to enemy breakthroughs. Since the introduction of the Panhard EBR 75 in 1950, France has led NATO in the field of well-armed, highly mobile recce vehicles. The latest in this series of French successes, the AMX 10 RC, entered service in 1978. Combining speed with killing power, this excellent armored car not only boasts a range of 500 miles (800 km) and a top speed of 52 mph (83 km/h), but also a 105-mm gun, capable of destroying all Warsaw Pact light armor.

Left: Serving with the British and Belgian armies, the Scorpion is a powerful light tank ideally suited to the recce role with its high speed, mobility, and powerful 76-mm gun.

Bottom left: The Spahpanzer Luchs 8 × 8 is very typical of the wheeled recce vehicles employed by NATO. With a crew of four, it is armed with a 20-mm cannon and a 7.62-mm machine-gun and is fully amphibious, having two steerable propellers at the rear of the hull.

Right: With a standard crew of eight, 122-mm D-30 howitzers can be brought into action within two minutes of halting. This gun remains in service throughout the Warsaw Pact.

Combat Vehicle Reconnaissance

After a protracted period of development, the British introduced the Combat Vehicle Reconnaissance (CVR) series in both wheeled and tracked variants. Powered by the tried and tested Jaguar 4.2 liter engine, the wheeled Fox has a range of 275 miles (440 km) and a top speed of 63 mph (101 km/h). It is armed with a 30-mm Rarden cannon, capable of destroying any enemy APC at a range of 1,600 yards (1,440 m), but the turret for the cannon makes the vehicle top heavy and liable to overturn. Equipping both armored and yeomanry squadrons, the Fox is also being issued to recce platoons of infantry battalions.

Although essentially a light tank, the tracked Scorpion variant of the CVR(T) series equips British armored recce squadrons and the Belgian Army with one of the most successful vehicles of its type in NATO's armory. Armed with a 76-mm gun, Scorpion is capable of destroying older Warsaw Pact tanks, using its speed to extricate itself from trouble. Its sister vehicle, the Scimitar, is equipped with the same turret and 30-mm cannon as the Fox.

The Bundeswehr relies heavily on the Spahpanzer Luchs reconnaissance vehicle. Equipped with a powerful Daimler-Benz 390 HP multifuel engine, giving it a range of 500 miles (800 km) and a top speed of 56 mph (90 km/h), the Luchs is armed with a 20-mm Rh 202 cannon, capable of destroying an APC at ranges

in excess of 1,500 yards (1,350 m). It is a highly versatile vehicle and likely to remain the cornerstone of West German reconnaissance for many years to come.

NATO now realizes the necessity to exploit every resource possible in the destruction of Warsaw Pact armor and many, once exclusively recce vehicles, are being fitted with antitank missiles such as TOW and Milan. So it is likely that in future, reconnaissance will be conducted more from the air, releasing the fast, lightly-armored, but comparatively heavily-armed vehicles to attack and deplete the leading echelons of the enemy armored advance.

Artillery

Warsaw Pact

During the past fifteen years the Warsaw Pact has dramatically improved its artillery. Until the 1970s, the vast majority of guns were towed and of old design, having first seen service in World War II. Also, fire control was hampered by an outdated system of

Artillery fire has always played a critical part in Soviet land attacks. Here the 152-mm 283, which would play a key part in supporting an armored advance, takes the salute during a Moscow parade.

communications which required the battery commander to be far forward of the guns themselves.

New self-propelled guns at all levels, a new family of command and control vehicles, better communications and improved fire-direction computers have improved the mobility and firepower of the Warsaw Pact. Artillery at regimental level has been tripled and a new brigade added at army level for enhanced versatility. Whereas in the past a surprise Soviet attack would have been totally incapable of incorporating more than half of nationally available artillery, NATO may now expect to face from the front line a 25-mile-deep barrage much improved in terms of both quality and quantity.

Top: Similar in appearance to the US M-109, the Soviet 122-mm self-propelled howitzer M-1574 entered service with the Soviet and Polish armies during the mid-1970s. It can fire various types of ammunition, at a sustained rate of five rounds per minute.

Left: Recently introduced, the 289 is a tracked 203-mm self-propelled gun with a range of over 30,000 yards (27,000 m); it lacks armor and NBC protection, but will prove a valuable weapon in the counter-battery or support roles.

Right: Vulnerable to counter-battery fire, and pushed to the limit in fast-moving advances, towed howitzers, such as this 152-mm D-20 have largely been replaced in front-line units by self-propelled guns, but will be retained in specialist and reserve units.

Towed Artillery

Towed artillery is rarely found in GSFG today, but the Soviets still prefer to maintain it within their rear echelon divisions based deep in the USSR, or simply to mothball it for use by reservists in time of war. It can offer many advantages, especially when used by poorly-trained soldiers. Cheap to maintain and easy to operate, towed artillery is usually light enough to be moved quickly over the worst road conditions. The Warsaw Pact satellites are rearming far more slowly than the Soviet Union itself, and will be retaining their old guns for many years to come.

The D-30 and D-20

Undoubtedly the most important towed gun still in service is the 122-mm D-30. Until recently the mainstay of regimental artillery, it is still used by airborne forces and has been exported throughout the world. With a maximum range of over 23,000 yards (20,700 m), the D-30 is highly maneuverable, can achieve a rate of fire of seven rounds per minute and is excellent in the direct-fire antitank role if required.

The larger 152-mm D-20 is now steadily being replaced by the 2S3, but may be retained for several years because of its nuclear capability. Capable of firing a variety of shells – chemical included – to a range of 26,000 yards (23,400 m), this gun is also highly accurate in a direct-fire role. Its size and relatively low rate of fire of five rounds per minute would leave it vulnerable to NATO armor.

The 130-mm M-46 has a range of 30,000 yards (27,000 m), increased to a staggering 42,500 yards (38,250 m) with the aid of rocket-assisted propulsion (RAP). Although primitive in design, it is likely to be retained in a counter-battery role throughout the Warsaw Pact.

Tracked artillery

Coupled with the new emphasis placed on speed and maneuverability, recent improvements in NATO ammunition and counter-battery techniques have made the Soviets realize the need for tracked artillery at all levels. The new family of Soviet guns share certain common characteristics and are all combinations of tried and tested components. The fully armored 2S1 and 2S3 also have full NBC-protective filtration and overpressure systems, enabling the crews to operate in contaminated areas without awkward protective suits.

The 2S series

The 2S1 122-mm self-propelled howitzer (SPH) was introduced in 1974 as a replacement for the D-30 in the motor rifle regiment. Using a modified D-30 barrel, it can fire the full range of D-30 ammunition together with a new RAP round, which increases its range to 24,000 yards (21,600 m). The crew of six, two of whom

The British light gun, a towed 105-mm howitzer, is of too small a caliber to be fully effective on the modern battlefield, but would still be deployed for airborne, air-mobile and out-of-theater operations where light weight and mobility are at a premium.

are transported in the ammunition truck, can maintain a rate of fire of seven rounds per minute. The chassis is amphibious, can operate in swamps and deep snow, and has a unique variable height suspension system enabling it to pass under low obstacles and decrease its target profile. Designed to suppress NATO antitank weapons with direct fire, the 2S1 can also provide a rapid smokescreen to protect advancing vehicles.

The 2S3 152-mm self-propelled howitzer first appeared in 1973 as a replacement for the aging D-20. Capable of firing all types of ammunition, including nuclear and chemical, the weapon has a road speed of 32 mph (51 km/h) but is not amphibious. The system will usually be deployed well forward in support of advancing armor, to be used in conjunction with the BM-21 in a counter-battery role should NATO artillery succeed in slowing the rate of advance.

The 152-mm 2S5 and 203-mm 2S9 are both useful new members of the Soviet artillery family. Although tracked, neither is armored or NBC-protected. However, both have exceptional ranges and it can be expected that they will be deployed at divisional and army level in support of all facets of the advance.

Ammunition

Besides having an impressive long-range offensive capability, all Warsaw Pact artillery units can defend their own positions at short range. At least five per cent of ammunition carried are HEAT (high-explosive antitank) rounds.

In the days of wholly-towed artillery, the Warsaw Pact expected its artillery commanders to go forward to a dug-out near the front line, taking with them their fire direction and signals personnel to direct the fall of shot by direct line of sight. With recent improvements in mobility, communications and target acquisition, the need for a more suitable command center

has since been realized, leading to a new generation of tracked armored command vehicles known as ACRVs. Now in full service with GSFG, the artillery command and reconnaissance vehicle (ACRV) utilizes the same chassis as the 2S1 and has existed in three variants since 1975. Not only does it protect the key personnel inside from small arms fire and shrapnel, but also enables the artillery battalion commander to exercise full control in a high-speed environment.

The Warsaw Pact has available over 24,000 artillery pieces of 100 mm and above, supplemented by at least 10,000 heavy mortars. Huge improvements have been made in equipment and tactics in the last ten years and the Warsaw Pact is likely to continue this trend in the next decade. In all roles, but particularly counter-battery, the sheer numbers and range of Warsaw Pact artillery will continue being a severe problem to NATO – a situation which is not likely to change very radically in the near future.

Above: Well-covered by camouflage netting as a defense against air recce, this Bundeswehr American M-109 is fitted with German breech and aiming equipment and benefits from an extended range over the standard gun.

Left: With only a 105-mm gun, the British Abbot lacks the weight of fire to be fully effective on the modern battlefield. It is due for replacement by the tripartite SP-70, if and when this finally completes development.

NATO

Despite a high standard of ammunition production, the sheer lack of range of NATO's artillery is placing the Alliance at a grave disadvantage. However, several proven pieces in the NATO arsenal are currently being rebarreled for enhanced range and accuracy.

Unlike the Warsaw Pact, which is presently developing a giant 240-mm tracked version, NATO has no heavy mortars, nor does it ever envisage using them. It seems strange that NATO tacticians who argue that the heavy mortar has no place in modern battle are the very experts now expressing acute concern over the large numbers held by the Warsaw Pact!

It is fully accepted that the role of artillery will be largely against enemy armor. Recent improvements in armor-plating have neutralized the effect of any shell smaller than 155 mm, making such artillery pieces as the French 105-mm Mk 61 SPH and British Abbot redundant, although both are still in service.

The FH70

The mainstay of NATO medium artillery remains the 155-mm gun in its various formats. The tripartite FH70 field howitzer is more than adequate in caliber and rate of fire and range, but it must still be regarded as a stopgap, as it lacks armored protection and realistic self-propulsion. There is a small fitted Volkswagen engine, but this simply enables the heavy gun to maneuver into position once unlimbered, and despite observations to the contrary, should not be regarded as a true form of self-propulsion. The FH70 is capable of firing six rounds of antitank high-explosive, illuminating or smoke shells per minute to a range of 26,250 yards (23,625 m); the US M549 RAP can be used to increase the range to in excess of 32,100 yards (28,890 m). A self-propelled variant, originally designated SP70 but now more realistically referred to as the SP90, has been severely delayed and may be close to formal cancellation. Doubtless its replacement will play an important part in European defense when it eventually enters service.

Above: Now the standard counter-battery gun in the US Army and serving with other NATO artillery, the M-110A2 lacks protection for its crew and can only equal the range of its Soviet counterparts with the use of RAP.

WARSAW PACT ARTILLERY

	D-30	2S1	D20	2S3	2S5	M-46	2S9
Caliber (mm)	122	122	152	152	152	130	203
Motive Power	Towed	Self-Propelled	Towed	Self-Propelled	Self-Propelled	Towed	Self-Propelled
Range (yards/m) (Indirect)	23,936/ 21,781	23,936/ 21,781	26,000/ 23,660	26,000/ 23,660	38,000+/ 34,580+	30,000/ 27,300	38,000+/ 34,580+
(Direct)	1,160/ 1,057	1,160/ 1,057	920/ 837	920/ 837	Unknown	1,275/ 1,160	Unknown
Rate of Fire (rounds per minute)	7–8	5	4	4	4–5	5–6	2

The French GCT

The 155-mm GCT self-propelled gun (SPG) epitomizes modern French arms development. Using existing domestic technology, the system was built primarily with the French Army in mind and shows little standardization with other NATO equipment. A good rate of fire of eight rounds per minute is achievable with the use of a hydraulically-operated automatic system, but only French ammunition can be fired and resupply might prove a serious problem. A full NBC system is fitted and the maximum range of 27,700 yards (24,930 m) can be considered adequate.

The US M109 and M110

The US M109 has been the cornerstone of NATO defense for more than 25 years, operating with the armies of Belgium, Denmark, West Germany, Great Britain, Italy, Holland, Norway, Spain and the United States itself. Despite being highly mobile and adequately armored, the original M109 suffers from a relatively low range and would prove no match against modern Soviet self-propelled artillery. It was originally intended to develop the XM179 155-mm SPH to rectify this problem – but when this proved impractical, it was decided to extend the barrel of the existing gun as a simple and cheap expedient. This has proved to be highly successful and the two resulting variants, designated M109 A1 and an improved version, the M109 A2, are now in service throughout NATO. Although the extended range of 19,500 yards (17,550 m) without RAP is not great, it does at least enable the weapon to compete in counter-battery warfare against the 2S1 and D-30 at all but the greatest ranges.

NATO's attitude towards heavy artillery is presently in a state of flux; in future more emphasis may be placed on the multibarrel rocket-launcher concept. Until this is fully developed, most members of the Alliance will continue to rely on the US M110 203-mm self-propelled howitzer. Nearly 30 years old in its design, the M110 has neither armor nor NBC protection, with a very slow rate of sustained fire and a dangerously low maximum range of 18,250 yards (16,425 m). It does, however, have a full nuclear capability and for this reason, if for no other, will remain in NATO service for many years. The United Kingdom, for instance, maintains one regiment of M110s as part of the British Army of the Rhine, allotting it a purely nuclear role. The United States has recently rebarreled the M110, extending its range by some 5,000 yards (4,500 m), and the resultant M110 A1 has been bought by several NATO countries. This should be seen only as a stopgap replacement for the equally old M107 and not as a weapon of the future.

Far left and left: Designed to destroy stationary or moving enemy tanks, a Copperhead round is fired from an M198 howitzer. When it reaches the vicinity of the target, its guidance system searches for a laser beam which is projected on the target by a forward observer. It is so accurate that it can drop down the open hatch of a moving tank at 10 miles (16 km).

The M107

The 175-mm M107 SPG, although no longer in production, is still in service with such diverse NATO members as West Germany, Britain, Greece, Italy, Holland and Spain. Built on an identical chassis to the M110, this weapon has a very long range of 36,000 yards (32,400 m), but is outdated in all other respects. The extremely long barrel makes the M107 not only difficult to maneuver, but also virtually impossible to conceal, so it must rely heavily on fire and movement to escape enemy air attention; despite its caliber, it does not have a nuclear capacity. The M107 is becoming expensive to repair and maintain and is likely to be withdrawn by all users as soon as replacement M110 A1s or the MRLS system become available.

Ammunition

The greatest hope for the immediate future of NATO artillery lies with the new and revolutionary developments presently being undertaken in ammunition. The American Copperhead and similar systems are designed for use against high-value, ideally static targets and can be fired from conventional artillery barrels. With a laser-sensitive homing device, the round is speared by movement within the wing and tail control surfaces immediately on firing. Simultaneously, a forward observer projects a laser beam onto the target. The projectile only has to be fired in the general direction of the target, is attracted by the laser homing device, and then guided onto the target. The Achilles heel of the system lies with the fact that it must be guided either by a member of the Special Forces or by slow-moving aircraft operating far behind enemy lines – and will therefore be very vulnerable.

With the advantage of systems like Copperhead and RAP, NATO has the capability of firing accurately at targets at the full potential range of its guns. The Warsaw Pact forces cannot hope to maintain accuracy at anything like maximum range to the same extent. The Soviet Union's ability to gain Western expertise is nevertheless well known, so that the Warsaw Pact may well be producing its own version of Copperhead in the near future.

NATO FIELD ARTILLERY

	PALMARIA	AMX GCT	M109 A2	M110 A2	LT GUN	FH 70	M198
Country	Italy	France	USA	USA	UK	UK	USA
Caliber (mm)	155	155	155	203	105	155	155
Crew	5	4	6	5 & 8	4	8	10
Motive power	Self-Propelled Tracked	Self-Propelled Tracked	Self-Propelled Tracked	Self-Propelled Tracked	Towed	Towed	Towed
Range (yards/m)							
(Normal)	26,246/ 23,883	26,246/ 23,883	19,685/ 17,913	26,575/ 24,183	18,810/ 17,117	26,247/ 23,885	24,060/ 21,895
(RAP)	32,800/ 29,848	34,461/ 31,359	26,250/ 23,887	—	—	32,810/ 29,857	32,808/ 29,855

Multibarreled Rocket Launchers

Warsaw Pact

With the introduction of the "Stalinorgeln" early in World War II, the Soviet Union was the first major power to realize the full worth of the rocket launcher and has since taken great steps to develop it as a weapon system.

The BM 21

The BM 21, probably the most successful rocket launcher ever, is held at divisional level as part of the artillery regiment. Three batteries, of six guns each, form a battalion. Capable of firing a 40-round salvo of 122-mm rockets in only 20 seconds, the weapon can also fire salvos or single rounds. Mounted on the extremely versatile Ural-375D truck, the BM 21 can follow tracked vehicles through almost any terrain, and with a maximum speed of 48 mph (77 km/h) can maintain contact with all but the fastest wheeled vehicles. Capable of laying down indirect fire at a range of 21,500 yards (19,350 m), either high explosive or chemical rockets, or a combination, can be fired. Thus with a single salvo, the BM 21 can destroy an enemy's nuclear protection with high explosive, whilst simultaneously destroying enemy personnel. Although equivalents are fast being developed, NATO does not have this ability to date.

The only weakness of the BM 21 is resupply. It takes the five-man crew ten minutes to reload, whilst usually no more than three full reloads accompany the launcher. It is far more likely that the BM 21 will be incapacitated by its own lack of ammunition than by enemy action.

The Czech M-70

The problem of reloading after each fire mission was solved in part by the Czechs, who introduced the M-70 in 1972. This system consists of a BM 21 launching apparatus, mounted on a 10-ton Tatra 813 truck, with an on-board reload pack of 40 rockets. Reload time is thus reduced to five minutes, but the resupply problem remains just as acute. The Tatra has the same road speed as the Ural, but has a greater range and even finer cross-country ability. A full 40-round salvo fired from either weapon can effectively destroy an area of 1,000 yards square (800 × 800 m^2). The presence of such weapons in the vicinity could have a devastating effect on enemy morale.

The Soviet BM 27

The Soviets had limited capability of hitting enemy concentrations between 15 and 25 miles (24 and 40 km) behind the front line until the introduction of the BM 27 in the 1970s. The BM 27 is the heaviest rocket launcher in the Soviet arsenal, and can fire a salvo of 16 220-mm rockets as far as 43,000 yards (38,700 m) in ten seconds. High-explosive or chemical rounds are available whilst a form of improved conventional munition is under development. Mounted on a ZIL-135 truck, the launcher is extremely maneuverable. Reloading takes 20 minutes, and because the vehicle is likely to be found further to the rear, resupply is far less of a problem. Not only can the launcher place a massive and instantaneous barrage upon a target, it can also scatter minelets behind an enemy position to hinder its withdrawal. The BM 27 is currently found in the Rocket Launcher Battalion at Front levels and in the Rocket Launcher Regiment at army levels.

The Soviets clearly regard the rocket launcher not merely as a supplement to the artillery, but as a weapon in its own right. The BM 21 is in service throughout the Warsaw Pact, whereas rather surprisingly, the more advanced BM 27 is in service only with the Soviet, Czech and East German armies.

NATO

Until recently, the MBRL did not enjoy universal acclaim in NATO and it was only the West Germans who could boast of an effective weapon. However, by the early 1990s, the United States, United Kingdom and Italy will have introduced these systems.

LARS (Light Artillery Rocket System)

Although the Germans developed the highly successful *Nebelwerfer* in the 1940s, further development was necessarily

Far left: East German troops prepare a battery of 122-mm BM-21s mounted on the Ural 375. With excellent cross-country capability the BM-21 can fire a full salvo of 40 rounds in less than 30 seconds, delivering over 1,600 lbs (640 kg) of high explosive over 17,000 yards (15,300 m).

Left: While the Soviet BM-21 can take more than 10 minutes to reload, the Czech variant the 122-mm M-70, based on the same rocket on a Tatra 813 8 × 8 truck, can have a second fusilade ready in under five minutes.

Below: In service with the West German army, LARS-1 is a 110-mm rocket system with 36 tubes and a range of over 8 miles (12.8 km). It now has improved fire-control, ammunition and an updated MAN 6 × 6 truck.

One of the most significant weapon systems to be entering service with NATO, MRLS is able to fire a variety of different ammunitions to a range of 18 miles (28.8 km); it will help counter the Warsaw Pact's numerical advantage in artillery.

halted until the reforming of the Bundeswehr ten years later. After lengthy evaluation in the late 1960s, the Wegmann Company was contracted to produce the LARS system. Consisting of clutches of 18 barrels initially mounted on the rear of a 7-ton cross-country Magirus-Jupiter vehicle, and now a MAN (6 × 6) truck, this launcher can fire a combination of high explosive, incendiary or smoke warheads a distance of 16,500 yards (14,850 m). The rockets are of 110-mm, fin-stabilized and solid-fuel design. LARS is extremely reliable and easy to maintain, with a rate of fire as great as its Warsaw Pact equivalent. NATO supply lines will be far shorter than those of the enemy, so resupply should not present problems. However, the limited range of LARS is a great disadvantage and the need for a far more powerful system has been accepted.

MLRS (Multiple Rocket Launch System)

The Multiple Rocket Launch System (MRLS), in service with the United States and now entering service with West Germany, Great Britain and Italy, fills this gap admirably. Mounted on a tracked, self-propelled loader-launcher vehicle, based on the M2 Bradley chassis, and crewed by a commander, driver and layer, the twelve 227-mm barrels are mounted in two groups of six. With the aid of an advanced Inertial Navigation System, which enables fire missions to be ordered direct by an observation officer, the weapon can be brought into action within 90 seconds of stopping. Thereafter it can engage 12 individual targets within one minute within a range of 18 miles (28 km). The conventional M-77 warhead weighs 350 lb (60 kg) and contains 644 bomblets capable of creating havoc against an unprotected target. West Germany and Italy will also be operating the AT-2 rocket capable of splitting into seven individual submunitions approximately half a mile (0.8 km) from the target. Each submunition will thereafter fall to the ground with the aid of a parachute, and is capable of destroying a tank.

Whether the MRLS is deployed forward to be used against enemy concentrations, as is the British intention, or further to the rear to destroy enemy tank concentrations, as is the West German intention, there can be no doubt that the weapon will add considerably to NATO's resources.

Antitank Weapons

Warsaw Pact

The Soviet Union spent the three decades following the Great Patriotic War regarding the tank as invincible, after its great wartime successes. This theory was rudely disproved when, in the opening stages of the 1973 Middle East War, an Arab infantry force armed with the manpackable Sagger missile brought the Israeli Adon armored division to a halt. The Soviet military hierarchy was badly shaken, and in November 1974 held a military science conference, attended by 200 high-ranking officers and officials. After an unprecedented second conference in January 1975, the Minister of Defense, A. A. Grechko announced a complete change in Soviet tactics – away from the massed tank attack.

The Soviets had been experimenting with antitank guided missiles mounted on armored vehicles since 1964, but had refused to accept fully the worth of such missile systems. To have done so would have meant abandoning their faith in the massed tank attack. As Khrushchev admitted, after seeing an ATGM (antitank guided missile) demonstration: "It hurt. After all, we are spending a lot of money to make tanks. And if a war breaks out, these tanks will burst into flames even before they reach the battlefield."

Reluctantly the Soviets learned from the lessons of 1973. The manpacked Saggers used by the Arabs, though they had been successful and though they lent themselves to a defensive battle, would be of limited value in the kind of fast-moving, offensive actions envisaged in any future European war. All BMP- and BMD-tracked armored personnel carriers are now fitted with ATGM rails to enable Sagger to be taken forward with the infantry. BRDM-2 armored reconnaissance vehicles have been adapted to a dedicated antitank role, with tubes fitted experimentally to the Mi-2 Hoplite helicopter. The latest Mi-24 Hind D & E helicopters were designed primarily with antitank warfare in mind.

Spigot and Spandrel

Over the last ten years, new generations of missiles have been developed, and more will surely follow in the years ahead. AT-4 Spigot is an infantry antitank missile, equivalent to NATO's Milan, which has already been in service for about a decade. It has a range of over 2,500 yards (2,250 m) and is a marked improvement on previous systems. While it is relatively heavy for a man-portable item, it can also be fitted to BMD-2. The AT-5 Spandrel replaces Swatter and Sagger and is mounted on vehicles such as BRDM-2 and BMP-2. It has a range of over 4,000 yards (3,600 m), similar to the British Swingfire. Spandrel presents a big step forward and is effective against conventional armor, but may be inadequate against the latest MBTs equipped

WARSAW PACT ANTITANK GUIDED MISSILES

	AT-2 Swatter (Figures for the most advanced variants)	AT-3 Sagger	AT-4 Spigot	AT-5 Spandrel	AT-6 Spiral	AT-7
Missile Range (yds/m) Maximum	3,600/3,300	3,150/2,900	2,150/1,950	4,250/3,900	5,500/5,000	1,100/1000
Minimum	550/500	375/340	115/105	115/105	115/105	55/50
Warhead Type	HEAT	HEAT	HEAT	HEAT	HEAT	HEAT
Weight (lbs/kg)	11.3/5.1	5.9/2.7	3.3/1.5	5.8/2.6	8.5/3.8	Unknown
Guidance	SACLOS (Semiautomatic command line of sight)	SACLOS	SACLOS	SACLOS	SACLOS	SACLOS
Target	Optical	Optical	Optical	Optical	Optical	Optical
Missile	RF	Wire	IR	IR	IR	IR
First-Round Hit Probability (%)	90	90	90	90	90	90
Launch Platforms/ Units of Fire (rds)	BRDM-2 : 4 HIND A/D : 4 HIP E : 4	BRDM-2 : 14 BMP/BMD : 4 Hoplite : 4 HIP F : 6 Manpack : 4	Manpack : 4 BMD-2 : 2	BRDM-2 : 15 BMP-2 : 4	Hind E : 4	Manpack Disposable Tube

with Chobham armor. Spigot and Spandrel have times of flight of eight and eleven seconds respectively, and are far less vulnerable to enemy counter-action than earlier missiles.

Throughout the Warsaw Pact, a policy of dispersing antitank weapons amongst the front-line units has been adopted. The best antitank weapon is still considered to be another tank, so that the majority of ATGMs are allocated to the motor-rifle units. Tank- and BMP-equipped battalions are considered to have sufficient integral antitank weaponry without the need for dedicated antitank platoons. A BTR-60 PB motor-rifle battalion contains hand-held RPG-7, RPG-16 and RPG-18 shoulder-fired missiles, with a maximum range in excess of 500 yards (460 m), and includes Sagger- or Spigot-equipped BRDM-2 armored vehicles. Antitank companies are attached to each motor-rifle regiment, with a full battalion held at the disposal of each motor-rifle division.

NATO

The lessons of the Arab-Israeli conflict of 1973 were not lost on NATO either. Immediately, the coming of the ATGM was seen as offering salvation against the overwhelming might of Warsaw Pact armor.

Far left, top: A Polish soldier aims his Spigot ATGW (equivalent to NATO's Milan) using the raised periscope sight, which will allow it to be fired from cover. He is guarded by two colleagues, the balance of the three-man crew.

Left: A Soviet armored corps soldier in camouflage suit sets up a Sagger STGW during a winter exercise. Though obsolete, this proven missile is still available in large quantities to Warsaw Pact forces.

A member of the British Light Infantry holds a 84-mm Carl Gustav, used by the majority of NATO armies as an infantry anti-tank weapon and normally fitted with a telescopic sight.

Another innumerable variant of the M113 is the M901, mounting the sights and two tubes on the elevated unit for the TOW missile system. An additional ten rounds are carried and loaded from inside.

The Carl Gustav and LAW

The advantages of a weapon light enough to be carried by infantrymen as part of the section- or platoon-armament had been recognized since World War II, with the introduction of the highly successful American "Bazooka". During the late 1960s, several European nations replaced the Bazooka with the Swedish Carl Gustav, which is still employed as a principal antitank weapon. The numbers of this two-man weapon in service with the British Army have been trebled in the infantry battalions, each section of eight men having its own Carl Gustav. Britain, in common with other countries, has also employed the short-range LAW-66, a single-round, disposable rocket. This American weapon, designed originally for use against tanks, had neither the range nor armor-penetration to be used effectively in this role, but proved useful in Vietnam and more recently in the Falklands against trenches and other softer targets.

The British LAW-80 (and similar developments in other NATO countries) represents a new generation of short-range rockets, which will be brought into service with the British Army on the Rhine (BAOR). Although these will become formidable infantry weapons in the next decade, they will not have the capability to take on the frontal armor of today's MBTs, especially those equipped with Chobham-type armor.

The Milan

For the NATO infantryman, the most important innovation in antitank warfare has been the Milan. A rare example of successful European standardization, the weapon was jointly developed by France and Germany and is now in service with seven of NATO's members. It is simple for its two-man crew to operate, has a night-time capability, with the addition of a TI device, and has a range of over 2,000 yards (1,800 m). Milan is also increasingly being seen as a potential turret-mounted system for APCs and other armored vehicles.

TOW and Swingfire

Ideally, heavier ATGMs should have a warhead capable of destroying an enemy tank with a range well beyond the range of the tank's gun, and should be fully mobile. In fact, NATO deploys several vehicle-mounted systems possessing all these capabilities. For instance, the British Swingfire, mounted on such converted APCs as the FV438 or Striker, is in service with the British and Belgian armies. The most successful of this type is the American TOW (Tube-launched, Optically-tracked, Wire-command-linked) system, which has been mounted on many different APCs and is in service with most NATO members. Another successful development is the joint French and German HOT, seen on a variety of vehicles within the French and other NATO armies. All these can deliver a killer blow from 4,000

NATO ANTITANK GUIDED MISSILES

	TOW-2	HOT	SWINGFIRE	MILAN	LAW 80	COBRA 2000	SS-12
Origin	US	French/German	UK	French/ German	UK	German	French
Missile Range (yds/m)	4,000/3,640 213/194	4,374/3,980 164/149	4,374/3,980 164/149	2,187/1,990 27/24	547/498 22/20	2,250/2,060 450/410	6,562/6,000 437/398
Warhead Type	Shaped Charge	Shaped Charge	Shaped Charge	Shaped Charge	HEAT	HEAT	HEAT & Anti-Personnel
Weight (lbs/kg)	5.3/2.4			6.6/3.0		6.0/2.7	
Guidance	SACLOS (semiautomatic command line of sight)	SACLOS	SACLOS	SACLOS		SACLOS	SACLOS
Target	Optical	Optical	Optical	Optical	Optical	Optical	Optical
Missile	Wire	Wire	Wire	Wire		Wire	Wire
Launch Platforms	Numerous Attack Helicopters inc. Cobra & Lynx. Several infantry support vehicles inc. M2 Bradley.	Gazelle, Dauphin & B0105 Helicopters AMX-10P Panhard VCR Jaguar AFV	FV-138 Striker	Manpack Wide range of infantry support vehicles	Manpack	Manpack	Assortment of infantry support vehicles

yards (3,600 m) – well beyond the maximum effective range of MBTs, of about 2,500 yards (2,250 m).

The Achilles heel of all wire-guided systems, such as those described here, is that the operator must be in total control of the delicate guidance system before firing, and throughout the missile's flight. This, in the case of TOW and Swingfire, could be as long as 15 seconds. Thus the Israelis, once they had recovered from the initial shock of their losses to the Arab Saggers in 1973, began to direct their fire not at the missile itself but at the operator, to distract him for a fraction of a second – all that would be needed for him to lose control of the missile.

The Warsaw Pact's concept of mounting ATGMs on all APCs, thus carrying the antitank potential into every front-line unit, has now been followed by the United States, with twin TOW launchers mounted on its latest M2 Bradley. The policy has not yet been fully adopted by all NATO members, but this is likely to happen as soon as finance permits. In this event, the ATGM will no longer be regarded as purely a weapon of defense, but as every bit as offensive as the tank itself.

Air Defense Weapons

Warsaw Pact

The Warsaw Pact is now concentrating as never before on air defense. It is realized that if its armies are to advance at the rate demanded by tactics, they must not be hindered by the new

Bottom: Milan being fired by a three-man crew with the aiming and launching unit at left, showing the long probe fuse designed to give the necessary stand-off from the target on detonation of this widely-favored anti-tank missile.

Right: Possibly the world's most numerous anti-tank weapon, this RPG-7 is held by an officer of a US Opposition Forces (OPFORS) unit, who use Warsaw-Pact tactics and equipment to train the US Army.

generation of NATO ground attack aircraft that will be put into combat from the first hour of hostilities. Air defense must be mobile enough to keep up with the leading echelons, and also be capable of engaging the enemy at any altitude. The Soviets have not forgotten that until the advent of the SAM-2 system, and the resultant shooting down of Gary Powers, the United States was able to fly U2 sorties with impunity over the Russian mainland. So the Soviets are determined to ensure that NATO aircraft technology is never again allowed to get appreciably ahead of their own defense abilities.

Radar

Air defense systems rely on radar initially to acquire and track an approaching enemy and thereafter to target and home the missile. Warsaw Pact electronics technology lagged far behind that of NATO for decades and is only now beginning to match it. Many Warsaw Pact batteries of six missiles still rely each upon a single target acquisition radar. Whereas this would be ample to

Left: Seen here on a floating bridge site, a Soviet artillery man uses a hand-held SA-7 Grail SAM. The Grail has an infrared-seeking guidance system, a range of 6 miles (10 km) and a quoted maximum altitude of 5,000 feet (1,500 m).

Above: A Soviet Army captain supervises the crew of a mobile ground radar station. Obsolete by NATO standards, this will probably have been replaced by more sophisticated and effective equipment to control SAM batteries.

engage a single aircraft, it would prove inadequate against several aircraft flying simultaneously into a radar's arc of responsibility. If faced with more targets than they are capable of dealing with, many of the older radar systems are designed to switch themselves off rather than overheat. It is therefore conceivable that certain SAM sites would find themselves suddenly "blind" for the crucial period immediately before an attack.

A pilot's greatest fear is to be shot down by his own air defense missiles. Few soldiers of any army, least of all the conscripts of the Warsaw Pact, have the ability to identify an aircraft making a fast frontal approach. The concept known as IFF ("Identification Friend or Foe"), by which each friendly aircraft emits a pulse known to the air defense radar and is thus identified, is utilized by the Warsaw Pact but is not considered totally reliable. It is certain that returning aircraft flying over moving "friendly" columns suffer at the hands of their own comrades.

The SA-7 Grail air-defense missile

The most prolific missile in Warsaw Pact service is the hand-held SA-7 Grail. Fired from the shoulder, it has a maximum effective range of over two miles (3.2 km). The original infrared missile

Right: Part of a battery of SA-4 Ganef SAMs, which would be deployed to protect the advancing armor from the medium-to-high air threat. Ganef is thought to have a range of over 40 miles (65 km) and a maximum altitude of around 65,000 feet (20,000m).

Below: A potentially formidable air-defense system for the Soviet divisions, the SA-8B Gecko is a self-contained unit with radar and four missiles plus reloads. It would probably be used in batteries of four.

was unable to lock onto any heat source other than the tail jets of a departing fighter, and with a top speed of only Mach 1.5, tended to burn out while unsuccessfully chasing its fleeing target. An improved missile now in production has augmented propulsion, an IR filter to screen out decoys, and far superior guidance capable of homing onto any hot area of an aircraft. The warhead is small and more likely to damage than destroy an enemy, but the fact that there are an estimated 50,000 SA-7 missiles and nearly as many launchers presently in service throughout the world makes this a most important weapon system.

The SA-9 Gaskin and SA-13 Gopher

Air defense at regimental level is provided either by the SA-9 Gaskin or the much improved SA-13 Gopher. Mounted on a converted BRDM-2 chassis, the SA-9 is essentially a derivation of the SA-7 with a larger warhead, more powerful motor and modernized controls. Launched by an operator situated in the rotating base of the system, the missile cannot be fired until the target has been located visually. Several SA-9 vehicles may therefore operate together with the aid of an acquisition radar but, as pointed out earlier in the chapter, there are difficulties endemic to this.

The SA-13 Gopher first entered service in 1980 and is now replacing the SA-9 on a one-for-one basis throughout GSFG. It is mounted on an MT-LB chassis, with groups of four or six infrared guided missiles mounted in canisters on a pylon, and with a range-only radar.

The SA-6 Gainful and SA-8 Gecko

Divisional air defense is provided by the SA-6 Gainful or SA-8 Gecko. Originally introduced in 1967 as a mobile battlefield defense system, the SA-6 mounts three missiles on a converted PT-76 light-tank chassis. "Long-Track" surveillance, radar and "Straight Flush" fire-control radar are associated features. The far more mobile and highly developed SA-8 Gecko was first seen in the Red Square parade of November 1975 and is now in service throughout the Soviet Army. Large enough to carry two

Below: The Warsaw Pact relies on a sophisticated mix of air-defense systems. The gun element, provided by the excellent ZSU-23-4 shown here, would prove itself a real threat to both fixed and rotary wing aircraft coming within its range.

complete reloads internally, yet light enough to be air-portable, the vehicle mounts four missiles along with search, acquisition, tracking and guidance radars. A new version, designated SA-8B, first appeared in 1980. Armed with six missiles mounted in two containers, the SA-8/SA-8B deploys in batteries of four.

The ZSU-23-4 antiaircraft gun

Although 30 years old, the ZSU-23-4 is arguably the finest antiaircraft gun system in service. Found throughout the Warsaw Pact, the four-barreled 23-mm gun is capable of a rate of fire of 4,000 rounds per minute, but is usually restricted to 3,200 rounds per minute to conserve ammunition. With a total ammunition reserve of 8,000 rounds, resupply is a major logistical problem. Mounted on a chassis derived from the PT-76 and equipped with "Gundish" target acquisition radar, the ZSU-23-4 is lethal to all but the lowest-flying aircraft at ranges of up to 1.5 miles (2.4 km). This weapon system requires a well-trained crew if it is to be exploited to the full; for example, it was proved unsuccessful in unskilled Iraqi hands when used against the US-trained Phantom-equipped Iranian Air Force.

NATO

Unlike the Warsaw Pact, NATO does not envisage a fully mobile war and can therefore afford the luxury of relying to some extent on fixed belts of air defense missiles. The position of all main NATO installations, including airfields, is well known to the enemy, and attacks on these can be expected in the first few hours of any conflict. As a result, each installation is heavily defended.

The Blowpipe air defense missile

IFF within NATO is not advanced in design; neither is it standardized or universal. Certain systems such as the British shoulder-fired Blowpipe have no IFF at all. The Royal Air Force

Left: Carried on a BRDM-2, the SA-9 Gaskin SAM is thought to be based on a development of the SA-7 Grail. It can have an all-weather capability when equipped with the gun dish radar system. Gaskin is now being replaced by SA-13.

Top right: A Roland 2 missile, discarding sabots, departs from its launcher mounted on a MAN chassis. It will be used to defend the US air bases in West Germany under a purchase and manning agreement made between the two states.

Bottom right: From a camouflaged hide, a towed Rapier crew member peers through the tracker unit. In the background, the combined four-round missile and surveillance radar unit stands ready. In this form Rapier proved its worth during the Falklands campaign.

WARSAW PACT AIR DEFENSE SYSTEMS

	SA-4	SA-6	SA-7	SA-8	SA-9	SA-13	ZSU-23-4
NATO Code Name	GANEF	GAINFUL	GRAIL	GECKO	GASKIN	GOPHER	—
ALTITUDE	High	Medium	Low	Medium	Low	Medium	Low
RANGE (miles/km)	43.5/69.6	21.75/34.8	2.17/3.47	4.97/7.95	5.00/8.00	5.00/8.00	155/248
GROUND MOTIVE POWER	Self-Propelled Tracked	Self-Propelled Tracked	Man-Portable	Self-Propelled Armored Wheeled	Self-Propelled Armored Wheeled	Self-Propelled Armored Tracked	Self-Propelled Armored Tracked
GUIDANCE	Command/ Semiactive Radar Homing	Semiactive Radar Homing	Infrared Homing	Command	Infrared	Passive Infrared Terminal	Radar or Optical
FLIGHT SPEED	Mach 2.2	Mach 2.8	Mach 1.5	Mach 2	Mach 2	Mach 1.5–2	Unknown

has already expressed its disquiet at the idea of such weapons coming under the control of inexperienced reservists with little, if any, recognition training, in time of war. The RAF has gone so far as to regard areas in range of known Blowpipe positions as too dangerous to overfly. As a direct result, areas with this air defense surrounding vulnerable key points would be out of bounds to all NATO pilots in time of war, making their already difficult task so much the harder.

Blowpipe epitomizes the various types of shoulder-fired missiles presently in service. The missile is optically guided, unlike its American counterparts Redeye and its replacement, Stinger, or the French Mistrale – which all rely on passive IR homing. Despite its success in the Falklands War when pitted against an oncoming enemy, Blowpipe was found to be too slow when targeted against sideways-moving aircraft. This should be solved by the introduction of Javelin, which is now entering service. This utilizes the original Blowpipe missile with a more powerful motor, considerably reducing the time of flight.

Roland 2

A major upgrading of NATO short-range air defense came with the adoption of Roland 2 in 1980. Based on Roland 1, which entered French and German service in the mid-1960s, Roland 2 has the distinct advantage of being operational in all weathers. Mounted on the AMX 30 MBT chassis for France and the Marder chassis for West Germany, the system is now being exported for

U.S. ARMY

the US Rapid Deployment Force. Under a joint agreement, 95 systems mounted on a MAN chassis are being bought by the Bundeswehr to protect USAF bases in Germany.

The British Tracked Rapier

One of the most versatile air defense systems in the world is the British Rapier. Originally towed, Tracked Rapier has recently entered service with the British Army. Mounted on the US M548 chassis, Tracked Rapier can deliver a semi-armor piercing missile a distance of four miles (6.4 km) at a speed in excess of Mach 2. Although put to work in the most adverse conditions, Rapier in its towed version – which remains in service – proved to be one of the most successful air defense systems of the Falklands War.

Patriot

Despite the protracted time taken in its research, Patriot is proving to be the latest in a line of successful long-range American air defense missiles. Each launcher carries four missiles in its shipping container capable of Mach 3. The phased-array radar performs all the functions of surveillance, acquisition, tracking and engagement radars; it is claimed to be effective against all aircraft, whether or not protected by clutter or intensive jamming. Patriot's great enemy is its cost. Even so, Hawk with Improved Hawk will remain operational in Europe as a highly effective weapon system for some time.

At this time NATO can boast only one truly successful antiaircraft gun system. Designed in Switzerland, but adopted by the Bundeswehr in 1965, Geppard is based on an Oerlikon twin 35-mm gun installation mounted on a Leopard 1 MBT chassis. Capable of a cyclic rate of 550 rounds per minute per gun, a total of 620 antiaircraft and 40 armor-piercing rounds are carried. Geppard is served by the reliable Siemens tracking and search radars, whilst a Dutch variant, designated Cheetah, is fitted with Hollandse Signaalapparaten radars.

Having long admired the Soviet ZSU-23-4, the US Army has attempted to come up with its own version – the Sergeant York

Far left: The excellent American Patriot system, seen here with one of the four missiles leaving its container. Patriot is currently being deployed in the Netherlands.

Left: Although balance in air defense between guns and missiles is nowadays regarded as important, the German Geppard system seen here is the only effective one in its class in service with NATO.

NATO AIR DEFENSE SYSTEMS

	Redeye F1M-43a	Blowpipe	Chaparral M1M-72C	Tigercat	Rapier	Roland	Improved Hawk M1M-23B	Patriot M1M-104	Nike Hercules M1M-14B	Vulcan M-163	Geppard
Origin	USA	UK	USA	UK	UK	International	USA	USA	USA	USA	West Germany
Range (miles/km)	2.0/3.2	3.0–3.7/ 4.8–5.9	1.86/ 2.97	3.1/4.96	4/6.4	3.9/6.2	25/40	approx 46/73.6	87/139.2	3.1/4.96	1.86–2/ 2.98–3.2
Ground Motive Power	Manpack	Manpack	Self-propelled tracked	Wheeled trailer	Towed or self-propelled tracked	Self-propelled (variety of vehicles)	Self-propelled tracked	Towed or self-propelled	Static	Towed, wheeled or M113 mounted	Self-propelled tracked
Guidance	IR Homing	IR Homing	IR Homing	Command-guided	Command to line of sight	Optical or radar	Multi-target guidance	Phased-array radar & semi-active homing	Command guided	Radar acquisition	Radar or optical
Warhead	Smooth case fragmentatlon	HE with proximity fuze	M-250 blast fragmentation	HE	Semi-armor-piercing with crush fuze and HE	HE with impact or proximity fuzes	120 lbs/ 54 kg	Nuclear or conventional Frag/ Blast	Nuclear or HE	6-barrel 20-mm M168	2-barrel Oerliken 35-mm KDA cannon

M998 Divad. Using existing components, this has been a disappointing and expensive failure; with its recent cancellation the US Army is without up-to-date air defense for its armor and will have to continue with Chaparral and the M163 Vulcan Air Defense System. This presents opportunities to European manufacturers, which will be good for NATO standardization. But the argument supporting the relative merits of an all-missile, all-gun or missile/gun combination to counter the Soviet helicopter and aircraft threat will have to be resettled.

Helicopters

Warsaw Pact

Although slow to enter the helicopter field, the Warsaw Pact has always studied and profited from NATO experiences, particularly in Korea and Vietnam. Today, it can boast a series of designs at least as good as anything within NATO. With the exception of its specialist attack helicopters, all machines have been designed with a joint military-civilian role in mind, so as to reduce the cost of development. All of them can be seen in Aeroflot as well as air force service.

Initially, development was heavily influenced by Mikhail Mil, a Soviet engineer equal in all respects to the better-known Sikorsky of the United States. Production within the Warsaw Pact now centers on the design bureau bearing Mil's name. Unlike NATO, where at least five major corporations compete within the same market, the Warsaw Pact has brought together its most accomplished experts in one center with obvious advantages in cost and efficiency.

The Warsaw Pact sees the helicopter as having three distinct roles. The initial military role was based upon the need to transport key personnel to tactical locations and to maintain

Top left: The crews of a Soviet Mi-2 Hoplite and a T-62 MBT transfer messages during an exercise. This helicopter, though of early 1960s design, still fulfils an important function in the utility role.

Bottom left: The Mi-8 HIP is a versatile aircraft, capable of carrying heavy equipment or a platoon of soldiers. In any heliborne assault, it would be used in these roles. The helicopter can also be fitted with pylons for mounting different weapons systems.

Top: The Mi-24 Hind D & E is a substantial, heavily armed, heavily armored helicopter that could pose a major threat to NATO ground forces in any future conflict, whether in an anti-tank role or in support of a heliborne attack.

Left: First seen by the West in 1981, the Mi-26 Halo bears Aeroflot livery but serves with the Soviet armed forces as the principal heavy-lift helicopter, with a payload of 100 troops or 44,000 lbs (20,000 kg) cargo.

surveillance of the border. The first Soviet helicopter built to these specifications, the Mi-1 Hare, first flew in September 1948 and is still in service with Third World countries. The Mi-1 Hare had an exceptional maximum range of 360 miles (580 km) and good foul-weather capabilities, but it could only carry two passengers. It was superseded by the larger Mi-4 Hound, at one time the holder of several world speed-records, and ultimately by the Mi-2 Hoplite, which entered service in 1961. The Hoplite is still the standard utility and training helicopter of the Warsaw Pact, but today is built in Poland. The standard Mi-2 Hoplite is capable of transporting eight passengers or four stretcher cases up to 360 miles (580 km). A "widened" variant, the Mi-2m, can seat ten passengers.

The Mi-8 Hip

The workhorse of the Soviet transport fleet is without doubt the Mi-8 Hip. Since its entry into service in the early 1960s, more than 10,000 of these exceptional machines have been built and exported to some 39 air forces throughout the world. The Mi-8

The British Army Air Corps Gazelle is deployed as a light utility and communications helicopter and as the scout aircraft of the anti-tank Lynx squadrons. It is seen here lifting off during an exercise in Norway.

Top left: Mi-28 Havoc: impression by an artist from the Pentagon. Whatever final form it takes, the Havoc will be a formidable weapons platform in the air-to-air or air-to-ground role.

Left: Three Lynxs of an anti-tank squadron flying through woods on the plains of Germany. Equipped with eight TOW missiles, they would present a significant threat to any Warsaw Pact armored breakthrough in the British sector.

Hip is still in production and is operational with every Warsaw Pact member.

The Hip can carry nearly a whole platoon of fully-equipped soldiers, as well as over 8,800 lb (4,000 kg) of cargo, and can accommodate vehicles as large as the BRDM-2 in its spacious interior. Although designed primarily as a carrier, the basic troop-transporter variant (Hip-C) can be fitted with two lateral pylons for the carriage of ground-attack weapons. Hip-E, regarded as the world's most heavily-armed helicopter, can carry up to three times the offensive capacity of a British Harrier jet. It is equipped with a 12-mm machine gun, fired automatically from the helicopter's nose, and its triple-stores rack on each side of the chassis supports weapon mixes of 57-mm rockets, gun-pods and AT-2 Sagger missiles. In an antitank role Hip-E would be potentially devastating but its size might make it vulnerable. More likely, it would be used as an escort for airborne-assault carrier helicopters over enemy territory.

Heavy-duty lift is delegated to the huge Mi-6 Hook, until recently the largest helicopter in the world. The Hook was designed in the late 1950s and still plays an important part in Warsaw Pact exercises, transporting 60 troops or more, or vehicles and missiles, about the rear echelons. Such a huge helicopter would not approach too close to the battlefront unless its flight path could be cleared of enemy surface-to-air missiles, because it would present a fairly easy target.

When the Mi-26 Halo first appeared in 1981, Soviet officials claimed that it was solely for peaceful purposes and would be operated only by Aeroflot. Since then, the Soviet press has published pictures of camouflaged Halos unloading BMD APCs. The Halo is larger than the C-130 Hercules, has a 44,100 lb (20,000 kg) internal payload and a freight hold 48.75 ft (14.9 m) long, 10.4 ft (3.2 m) wide and 10.25 ft (3 m) high. It can transport two BMDs with their crews inside and a further payload outside. In fact, the Halo is so big that it could carry as part of its underslung payload any NATO helicopter presently in service.

The Mi-24 Hind A

In 1973, the Soviet Union introduced one of the finest attack helicopters ever. This was originally designated as the Mi-24 Hind A, but other variants soon appeared, including the Hind D & E, seen regularly on television footage from Afghanistan. Hind is armed with a 12.7-mm Gatling gun, four 32-shot 57-mm rocket pods, and four AT-2 Swatter ATGWs (Hind D) or AT-S Spiral ATGWs (Hind E). The latter also has fire-and-forget capabilities and a range of 4.5 miles (7.25 km) and both can carry two 250-lb (113-kg) bombs. Unlike American gunships, Mi-24 Hind has a passenger compartment and is capable of lifting eight fully-equipped troops, though it would seldom be required to do so. The Hind has no directly comparable NATO counterpart, though it is often compared with the American AH-1 Cobra. The Cobra, however, is much smaller and cannot compete with the Mi-24 Hind as a troop carrier.

For some years, the Soviet Union has been concerned by the destructive potential of NATO antitank helicopters, and is now completing development of the world's first true air-combat helicopter, designated the Mi-28 Havoc. Far smaller than Hind, and equipped with a new fast-firing gun, Havoc will be able to fulfill all Hind's offensive roles (except troop carrying), but will be much faster and more maneuverable. How many Mi-28 Havocs will enter service is not yet known, but already it is reckoned that this machine will revolutionize helicopter warfare in the 1990s.

NATO

Most NATO members use helicopters – and among those nations who do, seven operate (or intend to operate) attack helicopters. Used expertly, these should be able to destroy up to 20 enemy tanks each, before they themselves are destroyed. To blunt a future Warsaw Pact armored advance, NATO will need to rely heavily on the capability of such helicopters to reduce the enemy's numerical superiority. Many tacticians feel that future wars will be won or lost in the air and that helicopters, at present accounting for more than half of all flying machines, will play a key role.

Helicopter development is slow and expensive. At present, for a NATO helicopter the average period of gestation, from initial development to commissioning flight, is a staggering 13 years. Many designs are simply abandoned as being too expensive. There are currently 28 different types of helicopters in production in Europe alone, which is clearly wasteful of both time and money. While the Warsaw Pact has enjoyed unified production since 1947, NATO is still no closer to putting its defensive needs ahead of individual national manufacturing interests than it ever was – as the recent struggle within Westland Helicopters of Britain has clearly shown.

To be fully effective, future generations of helicopters must be able to fly and fight at night, to sustain damage from ground attack and to lock onto enemy radar. Ideally, a new helicopter must be versatile and cheap enough to attract exports, though few currently under development fall into that category. The U S Black Hawk, for instance, is three times as expensive as the Soviet Hip—while Agusta A129 Mangusta, with its excellent engine and antitank capabilities, has found no purchasers outside the Italian Army.

Gazelle

Despite its numerous problems, NATO still operates some excellent helicopters. One of the finest reconnaissance and utility helicopters in service is the Aerospatiale Gazelle. This was originally the product of an Anglo-French agreement made in

Above: The German Army's anti-tank helicopter is the MBB 105P, an example of the adaptation of utility machines to this specialist role. It is equipped with target acquisition and tracking sight and armed with six HOT missiles.

Far left: The first of the European specialist helicopters, the Augusta A129 Mangusta (Mongoose) is about to enter service with the Italian Army. It can carry a variety of weapons including rockets or anti-tank missiles such as HOT or TOW.

Left: While the rest of NATO has relied on adaptations of general-purpose helicopters, the US has deployed specialist anti-tank and ground support aircraft. The latest of these, the Hughes Apache, is seen here firing one of its 16 Hellfire missiles.

1967, according to which Westland Helicopters shared production for the British market. Later, licenses were granted to Egypt and Yugoslavia. Production still continues on a small scale today, and over 1,100 models are currently operational.

Gazelle is capable of transporting three lightly-equipped passengers or two stretcher cases. It can also be fitted with a hand-held 7.62-mm GPMG, a 20-mm Giat cannon, a side-firing minigun or up to six HOT missiles. Gazelle was not really designed for the antitank role, and would only be used in this capacity as a last resort.

Probably the most famous utility helicopter in NATO service is the Bell Huey, designed originally as a small machine for US Army general service. Subsequent variants, which were built under license by Dornier of West Germany, Agusta of Italy, Fuji and AIDC, featured many important modifications. Many "Hueys" (so called from the original HU designation) are armed with a variety of guns, antitank missiles and night-fighting equipment. The Bell Huey, despite its humble origins, now operates in larger numbers – and with more armed forces than any other aircraft since 1945.

Lynx

Among NATO's attack helicopters is the Westland Lynx. Better known as an antitank helicopter, it is also a formidable antitank platform. The Lynx is highly versatile and maneuverable; reaching speeds of up to 200 mph (320 km/h) and with a full payload, it has a range of 336 miles (540 km). It can also fly sideways or backwards at speeds approaching 80 mph (130 km/h). The Lynx can accommodate a section of fully armed men in the rear cabin, and in some discomfort – though troop transportation is not its basic role. Some go as far as to argue that the passenger area is unnecessary and makes the

A COMPARISON OF HELICOPTERS OF THE TWO ALLIANCES

	Warsaw Pact	NATO
	Mi-6 Hook	**Ch-47 Chinook**
Troop capacity	61	44
Cargo (lbs/kg)	26,450/13,225	24,100/10,485
Mission speed (mph/km/h)	156/250	159/254.4
Mission radius (miles/km)	203/325	115.5/184.8
Armament	12.7-mm machine-gun	—
Length (ft/m)	136 ft 11½ in/41.74	99/30
	Mi-8 Hip	**Aerospatiale Puma**
Troop capacity	24	20
Cargo (lbs/kg)	8,820/3,969	5,500/2,475
Mission speed (mph/km/h)	140.5/224.8	165/264
Mission radius (miles/km)	150/240	210/336
Armament	4 × 16 shot 57-mm rocket pads or 6 × AITGWs or 4 × 250 lb (112.5 kg) bombs	Usually nil, but 7.62-mm machine-gun may be fitted
Length (ft/m)	82 ft 9¾ in/25.24	59 ft 6½ in/18.15
	Mi-24 Hind	**AH-1 Cobra**
Troop capacity	8	Nil
Mission speed (mph/km/h)	208/333	220/352
Mission radius (miles/km)	225/360	359/574
Armament	128 × 57-mm rockets and 12.7-mm Gatling-gun	2 × 7.62-mm minigun or 2 × 40-mm grenade launcher or 1 × 7.62-mm minigun or 1 × 40-mm grenade launcher
ATGW	4 Swatter or 4 Spiral	8 × TOW

helicopter too big and vulnerable.

Earlier models, which are still widely used by the British Army, carried eight TOW ATOW missiles. The latest Mk III variant has a new mast-mounted sight and eight Hellfire infrared missiles with advanced fire-and-forget capabilities. The British Army, who is the principal user of Lynx, spends a lot of time with the helicopter in exercises designed to assess the routes that advancing Warsaw Pact armor would be likely to take through NATO territory. Lynx plays an important part in working out the best tactics for destroying such an attack, and will probably be kept in service till the end of the century. And Lynx pilots of the British Army Air Corps are among the most experienced in the world. The helicopter could yet have a crucial role to play.

Apache

The Hughes AH-64A Apache, designed to include all the very latest antitank and attack technology, is also the most expensive helicopter ever built. Equipped with PNVS (Pilot's Night Vision System) and TADS (Target Acquisition and Designation Sight) Apache has virtually undreamt-of night-flying capabilities. It has day/night FLIR (Forward Looking Infrared) and tracker and ranger lasers to enhance accuracy, and can carry 16 Hellfire missiles as well as a 30-mm Hughes Chain Gun, fired remotely from a ventral mounting. The US Army has ordered 515 Apaches, presently being delivered at the rate of 12 per month. However, although this highly advanced helicopter is superior to any rival in the NATO market, it may prove prohibitively expensive for the relatively poorer European members.

Puma

The first country to use the helicopter in a formal assault role was Britain, at Suez in 1956, but the full potential of "air cavalry" was not exploited until Vietnam when, under the control of Secretary

The classic Bell HU-1 made its reputation during the Vietnam War. Seen here is the CH-135 "Twin Huey," a later, twin-engined variant, in service with the Canadian armed forces. It can carry up to 12 troops or serve in a variety of other roles.

of State MacNamara, some 15,000 Bell Huey helicopters were made operational. Since then, cross-battlefield mobility has been practiced regularly by the Israelis and is now an accepted part of NATO doctrine. An early, highly successful tactical transport helicopter – the Aerospatiale Puma – first appeared in 1967 and quickly became the mainstay of the Anglo-French helicopter co-production agreement of that year. The Super Puma, introduced in 1974, can accommodate 21 troops or nine stretcher cases with facilities for three orderlies. An impressive external payload of 9,924 lb (4,501 kg) can be carried, enabling Puma to transport light vehicles or artillery pieces about the battlefield. Both France and Britain use Puma as a speedy way of bringing men and supplies forward and to remove casualties from the front. In these cases the helicopter is unarmed, but in other circumstances it can be fitted with either two pivot-mounted 7.62-mm GPMGs or a hand-aimed 20-mm Giat cannon.

Black Hawk

Undoubtedly the most dexterous combat assault helicopter of today is the United States' Sikorsky S-70. The first version of

this highly unusual helicopter family (the UH-60A Black Hawk) was designed in the late 1970s in response to the US Army's need for a UTTAS (Utility Tactical-Transport Aircraft System) for general battlefield-support duties. Black Hawk can carry a full squad of men and equipment, six stretchers or a load of 8,000 lb (3,630 kg), and can easily transport a 105-mm gun, 50 rounds of palletized ammunition and a crew of five. Since the early 1980s, ESSSs (External Stores Support Systems), which were originally unarmed, have been retrofitted to enable Black Hawk to mount 16 Hellfire missiles, gun pods or even the M56 mine-dispersing system. There are many variants of this highly successful helicopter in service (notably the USAF Night Hawk and US Navy Sea Hawk), while small numbers have been converted for air sea rescue, electronic warfare and target acquisition. Many European nations regard Black Hawk as too small and out-of-date, a view clearly not shared by the United States whc, at the end of 1985, had 900 helicopters in service and a further 500 on order.

There is currently much discussion both within NATO and the Warsaw Pact on how effective the helicopter is against the tank. Up until the Korean War the tank was considered supreme and unstoppable, but with the coming of a new generation of antitank weaponry its role was re-evaluated. Consequently both Alliances are presently producing a new generation of anti-helicopter helicopters. Any future deployment of these on a large scale might cause another major rethink. Certainly, the helicopter will have an important role for many decades to come, even if the airborne cavalry originally conceived of by MacNamara quickly becomes a thing of the past.

Left: Based on experience gained in Vietnam, the US Blackhawk is designed with battlefield survivability in mind. It is seen here taking part in "Bright Star 83", an exercise that was held jointly with the Egyptians.

Above: A Milan team of the French Army disembark from an Aerospatiale SA 330 Puma. This medium-sized transport helicopter can carry 16 soldiers or 7,000 lbs (3000 kg) of external stores, by day or night and in any weather.

Sea Power

A General Perspective

Warsaw Pact

"The Soviet Navy is the custodian of socialism and all that it has achieved in its past struggles. It plays a vital role in preserving world peace. Soviet ships do not pursue aggressive policies, neither do they interfere with international shipping. They do not compromise the interests of others or threaten others' coastlines with armed aggression." Admiral Sergei Gorshkov in *Red Star*, July 1984.

Whether or not Admiral Gorshkov's claim is true, one fact is certain: that, under the Admiral's control, the Soviet Navy has grown within 30 years from an insignificant coastal force to the

This naval officer will have seen, contributed to and benefited from the growth in size and prestige of the Soviet Navy since the end of World War II.

Now capable of operating in all the world's oceans, a Soviet Navy task force, including a Kiev-class carrier and two other warships, is replenished at sea by the Keila-class transport ship *Berezina*.

second largest fleet in the world. Moreover, this growth shows no signs of abating.

Until the early 1960s, the Soviet Union paid scant regard to sea power, preferring to rely upon its huge standing army for protection. It was, after all, the Red Army who had fought and won the Civil War, while elements of the Fleet mutinied with bloody consequences. It was the Red Army who, according to Soviet accounts, stood alone against Fascism in 1941, eventually not only defeating it but also liberating a number of neighboring countries in the process.

The small Red Navy was virtually destroyed by the Germans between 1941 and 1945, with the result that Stalin had few surface ships at his disposal to meet the threat of the huge postwar American and British fleets. Rather than rebuild conventional surface fleets, which were expensive and required the support of a large shipbuilding industry, which the Russians did not possess, Stalin concentrated on building a formidable, secret submarine force. When Khrushchev came to power in 1953, a great emphasis was placed on nuclear power and a series of experimental and highly dangerous, nuclear-powered submarines were built.

In 1956 Sergei Gorshkov, then a 45-year-old naval officer, who had served with distinction in the Black Sea Fleet and had attained the rank of Rear Admiral at the age of 31, was appointed Commander-in-Chief of the Soviet navy. The beginning of the modern Soviet navy dates from this time.

The modern Soviet navy

The Soviet navy has grown to meet its own very particular geographical, political and economic needs. Because of this, its structure is fundamentally different from that of any of its NATO counterparts. None of the non-Soviet Warsaw Pact countries

has a naval capability of anything more than coastal defense, so that the Soviet navy has had to take upon itself the protection not only of its own borders but also those of its allies. Furthermore, the Soviet Union is surrounded by land on three sides and ice on the fourth, making it very difficult to construct strategically feasible ports and harbors. Unlike several NATO members, the Soviet Union does not enjoy the benefit of ex-colonial ties around the world and cannot rely upon friendly powers to provide her navies with aid, provisions and technical assistance when far from home. True, she now has bases as far afield as Aden, North Korea, Libya and Cam Ranh Bay in Vietnam, but these are all threatened by areas of NATO influence. Nowhere in the world can Soviet fleets operate with total impunity.

If the Soviet invasion of Afghanistan was intended not simply to secure a vulnerable part of the southern border, but as a

means of destabilizing Iran, and ultimately to take control of the Eastern Gulf, then the plans have gone sadly wrong. For the Soviet Union is forced by geographical necessity to maintain four large, mutually-independent fleets. In time of war, it is unlikely that any of them would be able to call upon the others for support. Consequently, each has to be totally self-sufficient, leading to duplication and a huge – but inevitable – increase in expenditure.

The Soviet Union knows full well that European NATO relies upon the United States for most of its reserves of manpower and equipment, and upon allies around the world for its supplies of food and oil. To the Soviet Union, disruption of these trade routes would be crucial in time of war, yet it knows that this will only be possible if large elements of the Baltic and Northern Fleets are fully operational in the North Atlantic before the commencement of hostilities.

Left: With its reputation made during the Falklands campaign, the Exocet has proved a very successful missile mounted on aircraft, ships or as shore batteries – even on Royal Navy frigates.

Above: The Executive Officer of the USS *New Jersey*, one of the reactivated battleships of WW II vintage, relaying orders to the engine room of this formidable warship.

Overall, the missions allocated to the Soviet navy are as many as they are varied. It must conduct strategic strikes against enemy land targets while preserving Warsaw Pact integrity abroad. It must counter the threat of large NATO naval forces while protecting the flanks of its friendly armies, and it must protect vital sea-lanes of communication while trying to disrupt those of the enemy.

To attain these goals, each Fleet must adopt different tactics. The Northern and Pacific Fleets, to which all nuclear submarines (SSBNs) are assigned, would be concerned first with the deployment and protection of those submarines. The near, landlocked Baltic and Black Sea Fleets, on the other hand, would regard their own survival as paramount and would spend most of their time, initially, in securing their own approaches. Thereafter they would support land forces by using their own naval infantry to harass the vulnerable NATO flanks.

The Soviets rely on in-depth defense in the sea approaches to the Soviet Union itself. Initially, nuclear submarines would operate under the protective umbrella of the growing naval aviation force and the conventional submarine fleet. Soviet surface fleets would operate in small specific task forces, much smaller than those envisaged by NATO. An antisubmarine warfare (ASW) task force might consist of two Udaloi-class guided-missile destroyers, two Krivak-class guided-missile frigates, attendant hunter-killer submarines and air cover.

A typical antisurface warfare task force might constitute a Slava guided-missile cruiser and two Sovremennyi-class guided-missile destroyers. Cruise missile submarines and land-based naval aircraft would be used in support when required. Heavily armed ships, such as the Kirov-class cruiser or Kiev-class aircraft carrier, supported by either Kara-class or Kresta-class guided-missile cruisers and Sovremennyi-class guided-missile destroyers, might put to sea seeking targets of opportunity. Single nuclear-powered hunter-killer submarines would certainly be dispatched to bottlenecks, such as the Straits of Florida and Alaskan coast, to cause as much havoc as possible before their own inevitable discovery and destruction.

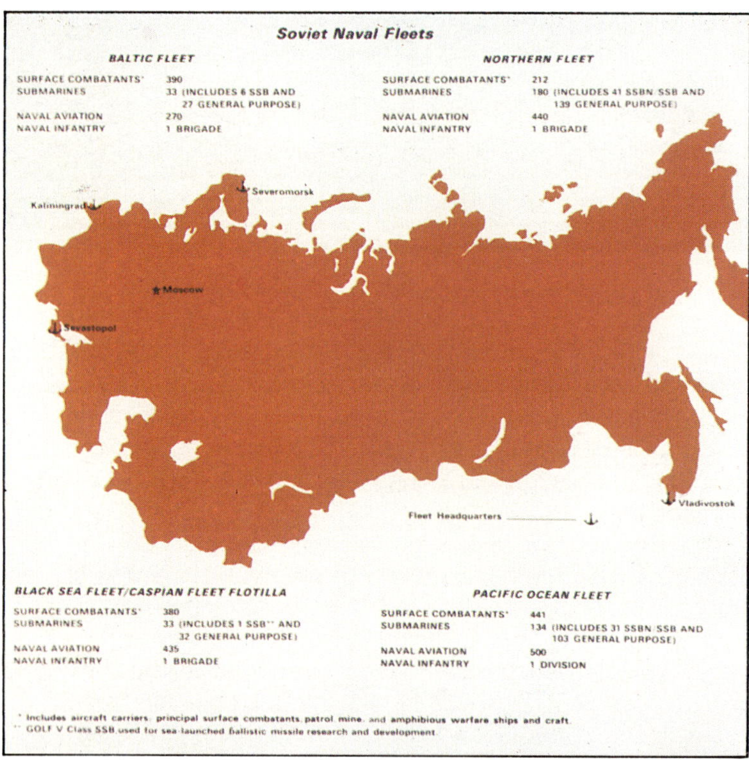

Above right: As a vital element of each power's nuclear strategic deterrent, the SSBNs constantly patrol the ocean depths with their missile control centers in a high state of readiness – as seen here inside the USS *Ohio*.

NATO

It is clear to NATO that if it is to survive in time of war, its merchant-shipping lanes must be kept open throughout. Traditionally, merchant ships have contained the submarine threat by forming convoys defended by small, purpose-built escorts. They would passively allow the approach of the enemy, with the intention of destroying them at the moment of attack. Although the principle of the convoy remains, much has changed since the introduction of long-range guided torpedoes and cruise missiles.

Studies carried out at the American Naval War College, Newport, Rhode Island, and elsewhere, have shown that defense of the North Atlantic shipping routes would require up to

Even in peacetime the superpowers play a wary game watching and testing each other. Occasionally things go wrong – as when this Soviet Echo II submarine collided with the frigate USS *Vogue* in the Ionian Sea, in 1976.

1,700 escorts – nearly four times the number available to the NATO navies today. John Lehman, the US Secretary of the Navy, said that his country might be willing to increase its fleet to 600 warships on a long-term basis, but hinted that this would depend on European members of NATO being able to reciprocate. However, only France and Britain have either the traditions or resources to do so, and both seem unwilling at present. France has always regarded the defense of the North Atlantic as the responsibility of the US and UK, and prefers to concentrate its attention on the Mediterranean, while the United Kingdom, as recently as September 1985, stated that it had no plans to build a new class of patrol boat for at least the next ten years!

In the words of Sir Derek Reffell, controller of the Royal Navy, the UK can afford either to build a new class of patrol boat, or embark upon a program of constructing two or three Type-23 frigates per year. New patrol boats would cost only one-third of the £400 million needed for a new frigate, with its helicopters, missiles and other weapons, but the Royal Navy has decided to speed up the building of larger surface ships to the exclusion of everything else. The Falklands war showed how vulnerable the present lightly-defended antisubmarine warfare ships (ASWs) could be to attack from long-range ground-based aircraft. Because of this, Britain will not feel secure again until she has completed the commissioning of a large number of well-defended Type-22 and Type-23 frigates, capable of operating anywhere in the world.

To complicate matters, an increasing number of NATO merchant ships are now operating under neutral flags of convenience and would not be easy to requisition in time of war. The British merchant fleet, for example, has declined from 1,614 ships of 50 million tons in 1975 to 1,141 ships of 35 million tons in 1980, thence to 640 ships of 16 million tons in 1985. The vast reserves of tonnage that made the huge merchant-shipping losses sustained in the Battle of the Atlantic just acceptable, are now no longer there. Today, in time of war, virtually the entire fleet would have to remain intact if NATO were to hope to continue supplying itself. Without the merchant fleet or warships available to sustain heavy losses that would result from the defensive use of convoys alone, it has become necessary to adopt a policy of aggressive warfare.

"Ocean Safari"

NATO now trains in the use of large aircraft-carrier and battleship assault groups, each far more powerful than its Warsaw Pact equivalents. Several such groups were exercised during "Ocean Safari '85", a major exercise called by Supreme Allied Commander Atlantic (SACLANT) Admiral Wesley L.

McDonald, in the fall of 1985. A multinational battle group led by the 15-inch-gunned battleship USS *Iowa*, and a carrier battle group including the US carriers *America, Eisenhower, Saratoga* and HMS *Illustrious,* were engaged in insuring the free use of the North Atlantic, while USS *America* and the amphibious assault ship USS *Nassau* sailed into the Norwegian Sea to continue the exercise.

During the decade before "Ocean Safari", US carriers had spent only 33 days sailing in the Norwegian Sea, but clearly the policy of regarding the defense of this area as too expensive has now changed. If an amphibious task force were to operate in these waters in time of war, not only would it need considerable ASW (antisubmarine warfare) support, but also its air cover would have to be supplemented by land-based interceptors. The resulting force would then be five times greater than anything previously envisaged for the defense of the area.

SACLANT, which is currently at half strength, does not have the resources to supply so large a force while undertaking other major commitments. One of these, containing the Soviet Baltic fleet and preventing it from escaping to the open sea, would inevitably lead to an early and crucial naval confrontation. The next "Battle of the Atlantic", if there is one, will very likely be fought soon after the declaration of hostilities, not in the wide expanses of the ocean itself, but within the close confines of the Norwegian Sea.

At the same time, a vital wartime task for the Soviet Fifth fleet, which maintains a permanent presence in the Mediterranean, would be to do everything in its power to isolate Turkey from its NATO allies. Of course, such an action would be strongly resisted by the US Sixth fleet, supported by the powerful French navy, and early naval combat could be expected in the area of the Eastern Mediterranean.

Within the space of five years, NATO has shifted from a defensive to an offensive strategy. The UK, which once planned to sell its only modern aircraft carrier, *Invincible*, to Australia, now maintains three such ships. It is further considering responding to US pressure not to scrap the old laid-up carrier *Hermes*, which would otherwise be sold to India. France, too, is constructing new underway replenishment tankers to insure the continued resupply of her "blue-water" fleet, and by 1989 will have completed the commissioning of eight new C70-Class Exocet-armed ASW destroyers. The United States is recommissioning several old World War II battleships while steadily increasing her fleet of smaller craft.

One of the 12 Forger-A VTOL aircraft on board hovers above the carrier *Kiev*. These would be tasked with destroying ASW and maritime patrol aircraft, anti-ship operations and reconnaissance.

The *Leningrad*, a Moskva-class helicopter cruiser, sails through the Channel – a single Hormone ASW helicopter is on the deck and the two twin 57-mm gun turrets are visible either side of the structure.

It is clear that under the influence of men such as Admiral Sergei Gorshkov of the Soviet Union and John Lehman of the United States, both Alliances are modernizing and enlarging their fleets rapidly. Any major confrontation between East and West would inevitably see early and violent clashes that would involve NATO and Warsaw Pact navies. The outcome of these would have a crucial effect on the war.

Aircraft Carriers and Naval Aviation

Warsaw Pact

The four ships of the Kiev class of ASW aircraft carrier are the largest ships in the Warsaw Pact fleet. Measuring 302 ft (275 m) in length, displacing 42,000 tons when loaded, and served by a complement of 2,500, these ships – *Kiev, Minsk, Novorossiisk* and *Kharkov* – are the only true aircraft carriers in Soviet service. However, the first of the Kremlin-class, with a planned displacement of 75,000 tons, is under construction in the Nikolayev Yards on the Black Sea and is due to enter service in about 1994. At present the *Kiev* and *Novorossiisk* are deployed with the Northern Fleet, and *Minsk* and *Kharkov* with the Pacific Fleet. In the event of hostilities, each will almost certainly be used in support of Soviet submarines within its respective area.

Antisubmarine helicopters

The primary role of these ships is antisubmarine warfare. Each carries two squadrons of between 15 and 18 Kamov KA-25 Hormone-A helicopters, together with a squadron of Yakovlev Yak-36 Forger vertical take-off and lift (VTOL) aircraft. The flightdeck is angled at 4.5°, but does not have the much sharper ski-jump which made the British ships of the Invincible class so famous. This is probably not so much an oversight in design as confirmation that the Forger is less versatile than the Sea Harrier and cannot perform rolling short take-offs.

In fact, the Yak-36 Forger has not been a success. Unlike the Harrier, Forger relies upon a series of three engines to give it vertical-lift off and horizontal motion. Originally it was thought that this would add to the stability of the aircraft during take-off, but it has had the opposite effect. The reliable operation of all three engines is crucial to Forger's stability during take-off, but the probability of failure in any one of them at this time is seven times greater than with the single-system Harrier. The situation is complicated by the fact that the two lift engines are shut down during horizontal flight and must be relit prior to landing. Unlike Harrier, Forger can only take off vertically. A successful deployment of Forger takes a minimum of 90 seconds (three times longer than Sea Harrier), making rapid deployment impossible. Furthermore, Forger expends ten times the fuel used by Harrier during take-off, to the obvious detriment of its range and, in all probability, would not be able to operate at all in very high seas.

Air defense

Air defense within the Kiev class aircraft carriers relies upon a combination of well-tried SA-N-3 and SA-N-4 missiles, with ranges of 22 miles (35 km) and 3 miles (5 km) respectively, supported by two twin 76.2-mm mountings and eight 30-mm point defense Gatlings. It is suggested that *Kiev* has been equipped with a new model of the SA-N-3 with double the range of the original, and that *Novorossiisk* has a new short-range SAM system, but this is unconfirmed. These fairly old defenses would be no real match for a concerted attack delivered by US carrier-borne fighter-bombers. The Soviets would therefore be forced to operate a large and costly defensive mantle of air-defense shipping around each of its valuable carriers whenever these come within likely contact range of an enemy battle group.

Helicopter cruisers

The helicopter cruiser is virtually unique to the Soviet Union. Until the mid-1960s, the Warsaw Pact saw as its greatest threat long-range nuclear aircraft such as the US A-3 Skywarrior, and concentrated all its efforts on the development of missile-cruisers able to destroy the carriers that launched Skywarrior. The introduction of the USS *George Washington*, the first Polaris submarine, in 1960, altered the threat overnight. By 1963, the

Above: A Soviet Kiev-class ASW aircraft carrier, the *Novorossiisk*, at sea in the Atlantic. It carries a wide range of guns and missiles in addition to Forger and Hormone aircraft.

Right: The Grumman E-2 Hawkeye, with a radar radius of 300 miles (480 km), provides the US fleet with the airborne early-warning capability that the Royal Navy lacked to their cost during the Falklands campaign.

United States had scrapped its Skywarrior nuclear program, had commissioned nine further Polaris submarines and had 31 boats of the Lafayette-class on order. The Polaris missiles had a range of only 1,875 miles (3,017 km), which meant that attacks on Soviet cities would have to be made from ships based in the Eastern Mediterranean. At that time Soviet antisubmarine warfare was the responsibility of coastal forces incapable of taking on any additional role. With the helicopter cruiser, the urgent need for a ship capable of both defending itself and destroying enemy submarines was realized.

Moskva and *Leningrad*

In the early 1960s, France built the *Jeanne d'Arc* and Italy the *Vittorio Veneto* and it was to these that the Soviets looked for inspiration. Both ships were hybrids, having large flight decks and hangars for helicopters in the rear as well as conventional cruiser weapons forward. The Soviet variants, the *Moskva* and *Leningrad*, entered service in 1977 and 1978 respectively. Much larger than their older NATO counterparts, each ship is capable of embarking up to 14 Ka-25 Hormone-A helicopters. Conventional antisubmarine weaponry is supplied by a twin SUW-N-1 launcher and two 12-barreled RBU 6000 rocket launchers situated in the bows. Antiaircraft protection is provided by two twin SA-N-3 launchers and two twin 57-mm guns. Unfortunately for the Soviets, the introduction of their helicopter cruisers coincided with the development of the US A-3 missile, with its extended range of 3,125 miles (5,028 km). This made it unnecessary to keep the Polaris submarines in the exposed waters of the Mediterranean and they were withdrawn to safer waters. The Soviet helicopter cruisers were thus robbed of their prime targets.

Although NATO, particularly France, operates a number of submarines in the Mediterranean, in any future war the *Moskva* and *Leningrad* would find themselves more hunted than hunting. Ill-equipped to venture far into the Atlantic, they could scarcely survive the might of the United States Sixth Fleet, supplemented as it would be by two French carriers. At present, the two ships alternate between the Black Sea and the Mediterranean, rarely venturing west of Gibraltar.

Hormone

The Ka-25 Hormone-A helicopter, purpose-built for the *Kiev* and *Leningrad,* is larger than the Lynx carried by Western European frigates and destroyers, but much smaller than the carrier-borne Sea King. It does, however, have a sizable weapons bay and is equipped for night- and foul-weather operations. It has a Magnetic Anomaly Detector (MAD) pod and is regarded by NATO submarines as a formidable enemy.

Haze

The Mil Mi-14 Haze, a variant of the highly successful Mi-8 Hip, is in limited service as an amphibious shore-based helicopter with the naval air forces of the Soviet Union, Bulgaria and East Germany. Capable of limited operational performance off water, Haze exists in antisubmarine and mine-countermeasure variants. Despite its fine pedigree, the usefulness of this helicopter is severely curtailed by its having to operate so close to land, and it is estimated that less than 150 models are in actual service.

Soviet naval aviation is completely subordinate to the Soviet navy and, with the exception of Forger and Hormone, is totally land based. The naval air arm consists of over 1,600 aircraft divided between the four fleets. Soviet naval aviation currently undertakes the four basic missions of reconnaissance and surveillance, antishipping strike, antisubmarine and support.

Sea reconnaissance

Reconnaissance is undertaken by a combination of 45 Bear D

Far left: Like its Boeing counterpart, the Soviet Tupolev Tu-126 Moss, a development of the Tu-114 transport aircraft, provides airborne warning and control. However, doubts have been raised as to its effectiveness over land.

Above: The principle ASW helicopter for the Soviet Navy is the Kamov Ka-25 Hormone, seen here over the Pacific Ocean. It is used on a variety of ships including Kiev, Kirov and Minsk classes.

Left: The Tupolev Tu-142 Bear-D. With an unrefuelled combat radius of over 1,800 miles (2,880 km), it is equipped with radars in the nose and underbelly radomes to search for targets and control ship-launched missiles.

turbo prop aircraft, 100 twin-jet Badger aircraft and a number of old May and Mail maritime patrol aircraft. The Soviet fleets rely heavily on the information gleaned from these aircraft, but intelligence-gathering is hampered by the comparatively antiquated and unreliable electronic equipment available. Until a new generation of sensors is introduced, a Soviet commander will always be at a distinct disadvantage compared with his NATO opposite who will certainly have a far better appreciation of the overall situation.

Antiship strike forces

Antiship strike is the responsibility of the fleet of more than 100 Backfire variable-geometry supersonic jets, supported by 220 or more twin-jet Badgers, each fitted to carry one or two of several types of antiship cruise missiles with "stand-off" ranges of between 55 and 250 miles (90-400 km). Certain of these missiles, such as the AS-2 Kipper, are now virtually obsolete, but others are highly sophisticated, operating variable flight-paths to help penetrate ship defenses. All are assessed to be nuclear-capable and carry a warhead of between 1,000 and 2,000 lb (450-900 kg). The huge range of Backfire has recently been increased by the introduction of in-flight refuelling, and it is now considered feasible for such an aircraft to launch an AS-4 Kitchen missile with a range of 190 miles (300 km) against a target close to the United States eastern seaboard. Approximately 75 Fitter C fighter-bombers have been introduced into the Baltic and Pacific Fleets, which would be used in an antishipping role in support of amphibious landings if needed. In addition to Soviet naval aviation aircraft armed with antiship missiles – Backfire, Bear, Badger and Blinder – aircraft of the Soviet air force often participate in naval exercises and could be expected to supplement the others should the opportunity of attacking a NATO task force present itself.

Submarine detection

The Soviet Navy operates a large force of aircraft dedicated to submarine detection and attack. Approximately 60 Bear F ASW aircraft, 50 Mail turboprops and 100 Mail "flying boats" operate a

Top right: A Phoenix AAM is launched from a Grumman F-14 Tomcat from USS *Constellation* – such a combination of an unequalled missile and an outstanding aircraft provides any task force with exceptional air-cover.

Bottom right: The British Nimrod AEW Mk 3, potentially a marked improvement over Boeing's E3A Sentry AWACS, has been dogged by technical problems and major budget overruns which threaten to end its development.

USS *Kitty Hawk*, shown here at sea in the Pacific, is a conventionally powered multipurpose aircraft carrier tasked with both attack and antisubmarine roles, for which she carries both fixed and rotary wing aircraft.

NG
101
NAVY

dual role of detection and destruction. On the face of it, these aircraft are equipped with all the futuristic aids to be found in NATO intelligence-gatherers, but much of their technology is outdated. For instance, while Soviet dunking sonar may be able to detect something lying on the bottom of the ocean, it cannot always identify it as a submarine, with possible drastic consequences if it makes a mistake. Soviet naval aviation also operates approximately 300 transport, training and utility aircraft of different types, undertakes its own training and is responsible for its own logistics.

Currently the Soviets are hampered by their inability to operate the latest generation of fighter aircraft from their carriers. It seems certain, however, that once the Kremlin-class carriers enter service, they will deploy the futuristic SU-27 and this obstacle will be removed. Until then, their potential remains severely limited.

NATO

NATO's strike capability is centered upon the 12 huge United States fleet aircraft carriers. France, the United Kingdom, Italy and Spain also have ships designated as aircraft carriers, but none of these is capable of launching fast, modern jets and it

Below: Tasked with maritime reconnaissance and strike missions, the Panavia Tornado of the German *Marineflieger* will pose a major threat to Warsaw Pact naval operations in the North Sea and Baltic.

Right: A Dassault-Breguet Super Etendard lands on the deck of the *Foch*. As the British learnt, this is a very effective aircraft when armed with Exocet – and it provides the strike capability of the French aircraft carriers.

would therefore be better to regard them as antisubmarine warfare vessels or commando carriers. Prior to recent hostilities in the Middle East, the United States carriers were divided between the Pacific and Atlantic fleets, with two ships from the Pacific forward deployed to the Seventh Fleet off Japan and two from the Atlantic deployed to the Sixth Fleet in the Mediterranean. Apart from USS *Midway,* which is permanently based in Yokosuka, Japan, the ships were each deployed on a six-months rota. Lately, however, events in the Gulf have

Left: The first commercial jet liner, the British BAe Nimrod, seen refuelling from a Victor K2 tanker. Despite being based on the Comet, it is arguably the best maritime patrol and ASW aircraft in service today.

Above: HMS *Invincible*, with six sea Harriers and a Sea King on deck, steaming at speed in calm waters off the Falkland Islands. During the South Atlantic campaign of 1982 she provided the desperately-needed air cover to the sea and land operations.

necessitated that two carriers, one from the Atlantic and one from the Pacific, be moved to the Indian Ocean, putting a serious strain upon resources.

If war were to be declared, it is the ships in the Atlantic Ocean that would bear the brunt. Very likely, operations would include providing cover for amphibious landings on the northern NATO flank, locating and eliminating Soviet surface threats such as the Kiev-class carriers and their battle groups, launching strikes against military targets in the Kola Peninsula, supporting the surface forces who maintain ASW cover patrols, providing air cover for convoys in the North Atlantic and – vitally important – securing the Norwegian Sea. Mediterranean-based carriers would see their main objective as hunting down and destroying Moskva-class helicopter cruisers and bottling up the Black Sea Fleet.

Clearly, these tasks would stretch available US resources to the full. Among other things, it is likely that two of the six carriers notionally available in the Atlantic would be undergoing refit or repair, making the job of the remaining four almost impossible. Two carriers of the Pacific Fleet might be moved to Japanese waters to harass the Soviet Fleet in Vladivostok, allowing the release of reinforcements to the Atlantic. But it would be some weeks before these reinforcements reached the Panama Canal and were in a position to play an influential role in the European theater.

Carrier-attack squadrons

The offensive capability of a US carrier lies in its squadrons of attack aircraft. These consist of two 12-plane squadrons of A-7 Corsairs and a third, 10-plane squadron of all-weather A-6 Intruders. Four A-6 tankers are carried in support, considerably lengthening the range of the aircraft and allowing strikes to be

Below: Showing a configuration of armaments based on experience from the Falklands campaign, the nearest of this pair of Sea Harriers carries four Sidewinder AAMs and two 30-mm Aden cannon to provide air defense to the fleet.

Right: A Lynx helicopter from the Type 22 frigate, HMS *Beaver*. Also serving with the French, Danish, Dutch and West German navies, the Lynx is the main ASW system on many frigates armed with missiles or torpedoes and currently being equipped with radar and sonar.

made against targets up to 575 miles (925 km) away. The EA-6, an electronic counter-measures (ECM) aircraft, might accompany an attack to jam enemy radar and weaken the missile defenses.

Four E-2 Hawkeye early-warning aircraft give advance warning of any air attack. This threat would be countered by two 12-plane squadrons of fighters. Certain of the older carriers still use the F-4 Phantom in this role, but the newer vessels carry the far more capable F-14 Tomcat. Fitted with the latest jam-proof radar, capable of designating up to 24 targets, a Tomcat can simultaneously launch six Phoenix missiles against different targets. In their fire-and-forget mode, these missiles stand a 90 per cent chance of success against targets 60-120 miles (100-190 km) away. Tomcat would hope to engage an enemy Backfire bomber before it could come into range to fire its Kingfish missiles. However, if this proved impossible, the Tomcat would zero its own Phoenix missiles onto the Kingfish itself, to destroy it in mid-flight.

Antisubmarine warfare

Antisubmarine protection is provided by a squadron of 10 S-3 Viking ASW aircraft, capable of identifying and locating the position of an enemy submarine before it comes into missile-firing range. The carrier-borne Vikings would be supported in this role by shore-based, long-range ASW aircraft such as the British Mk II Nimrod, which can locate enemy submarine movements by the deployment of passive Jesebel sonar buoys. The British government has recently ordered a consignment of Stringray torpedoes, so that before long, Nimrod will not only be able to locate and identify an enemy submarine, but also destroy it.

In time of war, the United States knows full well that the Warsaw Pact would do everything in its power to destroy a US carrier. It is therefore surprising that carriers have no means of close-quarter protection. Originally, ships of the Nimitz class relied upon three Basic Print Defense Missile Systems (BPDMS), but these have now been replaced by NATO Sea

Sparrow missiles with a range of 11 miles (18 km) and Gatling-type Phalanx CIWS guns.

Shore-based naval aircraft

In addition to the carrier-attack squadrons, NATO operates a number of shore-based maritime aircraft. The British RAF provides a squadron of Buccaneers to cover the North Sea. Other Buccaneers operate with the ancient Shackeltons of Number 8 Squadron, based at Lossiemouth, Scotland, to provide a rather tenuous link in NATO's early warning system. These sturdy aircraft were designed originally to operate from the decks of carriers but lost this role when the United Kingdom scrapped its one remaining conventional aircraft carrier, HMS *Ark Royal*.

West Germany operates two squadrons of brand new Tornadoes from Jutland. Equipped with the powerful Kormorant antishipping missile, these aircraft would be equally well placed to intervene in the North Sea or the Baltic, should the Warsaw Pact attempt an amphibious landing in either area.

The Norwegians operate a squadron of aging F-104 Starfighters from Bode. These comparatively unsophisticated aircraft could not match the latest Soviet interceptors, but they could at least make any landing on the Norwegian coast prohibitively expensive in terms of lives and equipment.

Long-range ASW

The prime role of most NATO maritime aircraft is the long-range ASW patrol. The United States operates 37 squadrons of P-3 Orions of which 13 are in reserve. Of the front-line squadrons, 13 operate from the East Coast, patrolling via the NATO bases at Keflavik in Iceland and Sigonella in Sicily, while the rest patrol the Pacific from the West Coast, Japan and Hawaii. Britain operates four squadrons of Nimrods, three from Kinloss in

Left: The Westland Sea King Mk 2 AEW is the world's first airborne early warning helicopter. It was developed in a record time of 11 weeks to provide desperately needed AEW for the Royal Navy in the South Atlantic.

Above: A prototype of the Dassault-Brequet Atlantique crosses the French coast. This aircraft is an update, incorporating major improvements in mission avionics into the original Atlantic model that serves with a number of NATO countries.

A Sikorsky SH-60 Seahawk crosses the stern of the guided missile frigate USS *Crommelin*. It is designed for both anti-submarine warfare and anti-ship surveillance and targeting, as well as for the usual helicopter roles of SAR and medevac.

Scotland and one from St Mawes in Cornwall, England. Norway and the Netherlands operate P-3 Orions and Canada operates a variant, built under license and designated the Aurora. The majority of other maritime NATO members operate the French Breguet Atlantique.

All NATO ASW aircraft carry sophisticated acoustic sensors, low-level television cameras, infrared detectors and MAD pods. The Nimrods and Orions have computer equipment on board capable of analysing data in seconds. In peacetime, patrols are normally unarmed, but in a war the ASW aircraft would carry depth charges and homing torpedoes and would be capable of attacking an enemy submarine within minutes of locating it. Unlike the Warsaw Pact, NATO does not operate vast offensive land-based bomber fleets, preferring to rely totally upon carrier-based aircraft to fulfill this role. In the days of their imperial might, both France and the UK operated large fleet carriers. Now that they have declined from being world powers to European powers, however, both countries have accepted that such large ships are no longer cost-effective or realistic.

The Royal Navy

In time of war, the principal responsibility of the Royal Navy would be the maintenance of control of the North Sea and

COMPARISON OF Ka-25 HORMONE WITH NATO ANTISUBMARINE HELICOPTERS

	Ka-25 HORMONE (USSR)	SH-3 SEA KING (USA)	SH-2 SEA-SPRITE (USA)	WG-13 LYNX (UK/FR)
Maximum weight:	16,000 lbs (7,200 kg)	21,000 lbs (9,500 kg)	13,300 lbs (6,000 kg)	10,500 lbs (4,700 kg)
Crew	2	4	3	2
Speed (Sea level)	135 mph (215 km/h)	165 mph (265 km/h)	165 mph (265 km/h)	170 mph (270 km/h)
Range (maximum)	440 miles (700 km)	675 miles (1,080 km)	460 miles (740 km)	425 miles (680 km)
Endurance	1.5–2 hrs	4.2 hours	2.5 hrs	1.5 hrs
Armament	1 or 2 400-mm torpedoes or depth charges	4 Mk 46 torpedoes or depth charges	2 Mk 46 torpedoes or depth charges	4 sea Skua AS-12 ASMs or 2 Mk 46 torpedoes or 2 depth charges
Sensors	search radar; MAD; dunking sonar; sonobuoys	search radar; MAD; dunking sonar; sonobuoys	search radar; MAD; sonobuoys	search radar; sonobuoys

western approaches. Since 1980, three ASW ships of the Invincible class have been built with precisely that aim in mind. Officially, each ship can carry nine Sea King ASW helicopters and five Sea Harrier VTOL jets for its own defense. During the Falklands War, however, twice the stated complement of Sea Harriers flew from HMS Invincible without any obvious loss of performance, and very likely this policy would be repeated in any future conflict. Ships of the Invincible class are admirably equipped to operate as convoy escorts or as the flagships of small ASW flotillas, but they are quite unable to defend themselves against concerted air or sea attack and, unless operating under the protective air umbrella of a United States carrier task force, would be highly vulnerable.

The two French carriers still in operation, *Foch* and *Clemenceau,* are both old and incapable of operating modern fast jets. *Foch* is now used as a commando carrier and no longer carries any fixed-wing aircraft. *Clemenceau* still operates one squadron of ancient Crusaders as well as two squadrons of Super Étendard strike aircraft, and a number of ASW helicopters. Both ships are deployed in the Mediterranean and, though out of date, would provide invaluable support to any United States carrier task force operating there. The Italian carrier *Giuseppe Garibaldi* operates two squadrons of Sea Kings in a purely ASW role. The ship is small and has a small crew, but its design is modern and it too could render useful assistance to a Mediterranean-based United States carrier task force.

Major Surface Vessels

Warsaw Pact

Construction of Warsaw Pact major surface shipping is influenced very largely by the knowledge that a future maritime confrontation might be nuclear. Under these circumstances, large carrier or battleship task forces would be highly vulnerable.

All Soviet cruisers (the Soviets are the only Warsaw Pact members to have cruisers) are designed with a dual offensive/ defensive capacity, and even the Kiev- and Moskva-class aircraft carriers have built-in air-defense capabilities. Large ships constructed in the last two decades have been designed with independent operations in mind. They carry an independent AAW (Antiaircraft Warfare) system and advanced ECM equipment. Their communications system is sophisticated enough to allow each ship, operating anywhere in the world, to maintain contact with its home base, through which all orders are relayed.

Below left: Now standard on many US ships, the Kaman SH-2F Seasprite is the latest variant of this multirole helicopter. It can carry radar, sonobuoys, MAD gear, EDM and torpedoes in its antisubmarine role.

Left: Kresta II ships, such as the one shown here, changed the role of the Kresta class to ASW. Kresta II, with its enhanced air-defense systems, is an example of the Soviets' ability to fit a much wider range of weapons into the hull than is found on comparable NATO vessels.

A COMPARISON OF WARSAW PACT AND NATO AIRCRAFT CARRIERS

	Kiev	Moskva	Nimitz	Kitty Hawk	Invincible	Clemenceau	Giuseppe Garibaldi
Nationality	USSR	USSR	USA	USA	UK	FRANCE	ITALY
Displacement (m. tons)	42,000 (laden)	19,200 (laden)	91,400 (laden)	82,000 (laden)	19,812 (laden)	32,780 (laden)	13,370 (laden)
length (ft/m) beam (ft/m) draught (ft/m)	902/275.6 157.5/47.2 33/9.9	625/187.5 112/33.6 25/1.5	1,092/327.6 251/75.3 37/11	1,073/321.9 268/80.4 36/10.8	677/203 105/31.5 24/7.2	870/261 168/50.4 28.1/8.4	591/177.3 100/30 22/6.6
Propulsion	Geared steam turbines 180,000 shp 4 shafts	2 shaft geared turbines 100,000 shp 2 shafts	Nuclear 2 A4W reactors 260,000 shp 4 shafts	Geared steam turbines 280,000 shp 4 shafts	4 Rolls-Royce Olympus gas-turbine 112,000 shp 2 shafts	Geared steam turbines 126,000 shp 2 shafts	4 LM 2500 gas turbines 80,000 shp 2 shafts
Armament	8 : SS-N-12 2 : SS-N-3 2 : twin SS-N-4 2 : twin 76.2-mm 1 : twin SUW-N-1 2 : RBU 6000	4 : SA-N-3 4 : 57-mm	3 : Sea Sparrow Phalanx CIWS	2 : Twin Terrier 3 : Sea Sparrow	1 : Twin Sea Dart 2 : Phalanx CIWS	8 : 3.9 in (100-mm) DP Guns	4 : Otomat Mk 2 SSM 2 : Albatross SAMs 3 : Twin Breda 40-mm
Aircraft	12 : Forger 18 : Hormone	18 : Hormone	24 : Tomcat 24 : Corsair 10 : Intruder 4 : Tankers 4 : Hawkeye 10 : Viking 4: Prowler	24 : Tomcat 24 : Corsair 10 : Intruder 4 : Tankers 4 : Hawkeye 10 : Viking 4 : Prowler	5 : Sea Harrier 2 : Sea King AEW 5 : Sea King HAS	16 : Super Étendard 3 : Étendard IVP 7 : Breguet Auze 2 : Alouette III	18 : Sea King
Complement	2,500	850	5,776	5,490	1,320	1,338	550

A Kynda-class missile cruiser refuels at sea from the *Karl Marx*. Launched in the 1960s and designed for surface warfare, they were the first ships of this type, marking the switch from guns to missiles.

The Kirov-class rocket cruiser

To some extent, all Soviet ships are general-purpose. The large ships, however, fall into the two basic categories of ASW and antishipping. Rocket-launcher ships were designed originally to defend the outer perimeters of Warsaw Pact seaspace against carrier task forces. The largest ships within this category are those of the Kirov class. Officially designated battle cruisers, they are, in many respects, still under development. In fact, the second ship of this class (*Frunze*) is so different to the first (*Kirov*) that many analysts do not regard them as sister ships.

The main armament of both comprises 20 SS-N-19 antiship missiles with a range of 290 miles (470 km), housed forward and fired vertically from individual silos. The secondary SS-N-14 antisubmarine missile twin-launcher found on the Kirov does not appear on the *Frunze,* having been replaced by two sets of four SA-N-8 SAMs. Also, the two single 100-mm guns at the aft of *Kirov* are replaced by a twin 130-mm turret on *Frunze*, and four 30-mm close-in weapon systems have been added.

Clearly the Soviets are more worried by the threat of the US Navy's air power than by her submarines, and have added as much extra air defense as possible. In so doing, they have been forced to employ several different types of SAM systems each with its own associated radar, making the whole operation very expensive. Future ships of the Kirov class will probably appear with new SAM systems now under development, to replace the hotchpotch presently in use.

The smaller Kynda-class cruisers are armed with two large SS-N-3 quadruple missile launchers, but have little in the way of air defense, relying upon ground-based aircraft to provide their protection. Interestingly, the later Kresta-class cruisers have only half the number of SSM launchers of the Kyndas, but instead carry SAM systems fore and aft.

ASW cruisers

With the arrival of Polaris, the Soviets began to concentrate on the production of ASW ships, at the expense of rocket cruisers. Among the latest ships of this type are the Kresta II-class cruisers, converted originally from Kresta rocket cruisers. The original antiship missiles have been replaced by quadruple ASW missile launchers, and a more powerful sonar has been fitted. A Hormone-A ASW helicopter, equipped with its own sonar, is housed in the stern.

Soviet fear of NATO aircraft is again apparent in the design of the Kara-class ASW cruiser, which made its first appearance shortly after the Kresta IIs. Here, extra air-defense systems have been fitted at the cost of speed and range. Clearly, it is anticipated that US carriers will try to carry the air battle far forward to the Soviet naval bases, bringing the ASW cruisers, which defend the entrances to these bases, within range.

Left: Large and powerful compared with NATO standards, the *Kirov* packs a diverse range of weapon systems to attack surface vessels or submarines. It also carries air defense missiles and guns, which accounts for the variety of radars shown in the picture.

Below: Launched in 1959 as the first nuclear-powered surface ship and the first warship to have guided missiles as a main battery, USS *Long Beach* has now undergone mid-life modernization.

NATO

The NATO alliance is fully aware that the Warsaw Pact, in time of war, would see the destruction of the US carrier task forces as one of its greatest priorities. The threat would come, not only from missile-carrying surface ships and submarines, but also from land-based bombers. NATO has therefore perceived the need to build classes of support ships capable of defending the huge carriers from any contingency.

Guided-missile support ships

Originally, the US missile-armed escorts were designated "frigates", but in 1975 all but one of them were redesignated "guided-missile cruisers" (CGs). Responsibility for air defense was assigned to the Terrier area system, while the ASROC missile was introduced to combat the submarine threat.

The first truly dedicated, large support ships were the Coontz class, built between 1957 and 1960. Redesignated as guided-missile destroyers (DDGs) in 1975, these ships are armed with a single 5-inch gun forward, a single Terrier launcher with 40 reloads, a 20-mm Phalanx for close air defense, two triple Mk 32 ASW tubes and a quadruple ASROC launcher. The later Leahy class has a second Terrier launcher in place of the 5-inch gun, but in other respects is similar. The Belknap class have reverted to the single Terrier launcher, but carry vastly increased ASW weaponry out of growing fear of Soviet submarine potential. These three classes of escort, about 30 ships in all, form the backbone of NATO large escort shipping. They normally operate in pairs and, with a stated speed of 34 knots, are capable of providing a high degree of protection to any task force.

Nuclear-powered aircraft carriers

The construction of the first nuclear-powered aircraft carriers created new problems for escort vessels. Although conventional-powered escorts were fast enough to operate with the carriers, their range was limited by the need to refuel regularly. It was decided that, whatever the cost, a sufficient number of nuclear escort cruisers would have to be built. Between 1957 and 1959 USS *Long Beach* was built, the first operational nuclear-powered surface warship to be commissioned anywhere in the world. Recently *Long Beach* has been retrofitted with Harpoon SSMs and two 20-mm Phalanx close support weapons. The ship is also equipped with an octuple ASROC ASW launcher. Two ships of the California class, built between 1970 and 1972, have both been retrofitted with Harpoon, and carry the advanced Chaffroc Rapid Bloom Overhead Chaff System.

The Virginia class

The Virginia class, the latest US nuclear-powered cruisers to enter service, follow on from the Californias – but feature a number of significant improvements. A new twin ASROC launcher has been fitted forward, with a helicopter hangar built into the stern. They also have two quadruple Harpoon launchers

The veteran USS *New Jersey* most recently saw service in the Lebanon. It will still play an important part in any future conflict if equipped with weapon systems such as this Tomahawk cruise missile being launched.

47

and two 5-inch guns. A revolutionary new magazine layout, reducing the potential length of the ships by 16.5 feet (4.9 m), is a further feature, one that is likely to play an important role in future ship design. Originally, it was intended to build eleven ships of the Virginia class, but production was halted after only four had been built. They now operate in the Atlantic in support of the carriers USS *Nimitz* and *Eisenhower.*

The Aegis combat system

The introduction of the Aegis combat system into the newest ships in the US cruiser fleet represents a breakthrough in defensive potential. Before, there had always been the fear that conventional radar would be swamped by a massed missile attack, but with the Aegis installed, the problem is reduced considerably. Aegis can locate any enemy missile approaching a task force, assess the sequence of threat and engage the missile with a variety of weapons either automatically or by means of manual override. Working in conjunction with the new SM-2 missile system, Aegis can control up to 18 missiles in the air simultaneously.

Originally, it was intended that the Aegis system would be fitted to a new class of nuclear-powered cruiser, but the huge combined cost of Aegis and nuclear propulsion have made this impossible. It was therefore decided to use cheaper, conventional power and to build a new class of large cruiser that was capable of not only fitting Aegis, but also carrying sufficient SAM systems to exploit its full potential. The first in a proposed class of 26 such ships was USS *Ticonderoga.* The 9,600-ton Ticonderoga-class are designed to operate as task force flagships. They are armed with two SM-2 Mk 26 launchers, eight Harpoon launchers, two 5-inch guns and two Phalanxes for air defense, six torpedo tubes and ASROC for ASW. They also carry an elaborate "combat information center", capable of receiving and assessing intelligence from all ships and aircraft in the task force simultaneously.

Apart from the United States, only Italy and France operate cruisers, and Italy will soon be scrapping theirs. France utilizes three ships as AAW escorts to defend its attack carriers. The largest of these, *Le Colbert,* operates Mascura area-defense missiles and an updated-version gun battery. The ship's extensive radar and communications systems enable it to control aircraft while acting as flagship. Working in conjunction with destroyers of the Georges Leygues (C70) class, it represents the mainstay of a potentially very effective Mediterranean task force.

New Jersey and *Iowa*

Perhaps the most emotive ships afloat today are the two huge battleships USS *New Jersey* and *Iowa.* Veterans of the Pacific War in 1944-45, of Korea and, in the case of *New Jersey,* Vietnam, these 58,000-ton titans seem to belong to a bygone era. They are, however, very powerful fighting forces. Armed with 16-inch guns (three times larger than any other guns afloat), two quadruple Tomahawk cruise missile-launchers, and eight Harpoon launch cannisters, these giants far outclass the offensive ability of any Warsaw Pact ship. Moreover, their armor, built originally to withstand the 18-inch guns of the Japanese Yamato battleships, is capable of withstanding direct hits from all but the largest of missiles. USS *Missouri,* another veteran, is presently reentering service, to be followed in 1988 by USS *Wisconsin.* These much-needed ships are returning to service at a tiny fraction of the cost of new ships with comparable capabilities. A very valuable addition to NATO, they are a total vindication of the United States' policy of mothballing a large percentage of its decommissioned ships, rather than scrapping them.

Left: USS *Ticonderoga*, the most sophisticated escort available to NATO to counter a saturation missile attack. One of the four fixed planar antennas and the eyes of the Aegis system can be seen above the SAM launcher and 5-inch gun.

Below: The high accuracy and long range of the submarine-launched, nuclear-armed SS-NX-21 cruise missile adds another dimension to the strategic threat posed by Soviet forces, to be countered by NATO.

Submarines

Warsaw Pact

Apart from ten old vessels in the Polish and Bulgarian navies, all the submarines within the Warsaw Pact are Soviet. Since 1945, the Soviet Union has built more than 630 submarines of different classes, including over 200 nuclear vessels – and a further eight to ten each year are under construction. Not surprisingly, the Soviet Union is the world's leading submarine builder today.

The submarines are built in five different yards, including the huge White Sea complex at Severodvinsk, which alone is reputed to have a larger capacity than all the yards in the United States, Britain and France combined. Currently the Soviet Union is producing nine different classes of submarine, of which all but one are nuclear-powered. The program of construction spans the entire range of undersea warfare, including antiship cruise missile attack, torpedo attack, land attack SLCM (Sea-Launched Cruise Missile) and communications support. However, it would appear that there is now more emphasis on the development of a new class of small, ultra-quiet diesel craft, capable of operating in the close waters of the Baltic or Mediterranean. Such a craft would not have the destructive potential of a larger, nuclear submarine but it would stand a far better chance of avoiding detection by NATO ASW (antisubmarine warfare) ships and aircraft.

Today, the Soviet submarine force numbers approximately 380 units, of which about 200 are nuclear-powered. There are three basic categories of submarine: torpedo attack submarines, for destroying enemy surface or underwater shipping by the use of the torpedo or missile-delivered ASW weapons; cruise missile submarines, designed originally to attack large and important targets from extended range; and strategic ballistic missile submarines, armed with vertically launched nuclear missiles capable of destroying strategically important land targets. Obviously, this last category is of deterrent value only,except in the event of a full-scale nuclear confrontation.

The Mike-class SSN

The Soviet navy operates about 225 attack submarines, most of them modern and many of them nuclear-powered. Since 1983, four new classes of nuclear-powered attack submarine have been introduced. The Mike-class SSN is of a revolutionary new titanium construction, far in advance of NATO technology, and is capable of operating at previously unheard-of depths. At 9,700 tons it is also the largest SSN in the world. Little more is known about it at present, but Western experts believe that the usual 21-inch (53.3-cm) torpedo tubes might have been enlarged to accommodate the latest SS-NX-21 missile. The Sierra-class SSN, which like the Mike-class SSN entered service in 1984, is identical in many respects to the older-established Victor III class, but at 8,000 tons it is 20 per cent heavier, has a large pressure hull and can operate at greater depths.

It is clear that the Soviets now regard deception as a priority and sea speed as an irrelevancy. When the Alfa-class SSN entered service in 1978, it was easily the fastest attack submarine in the world (28 knots dived). Eight years on, NATO ASW technology had developed so far that the Soviets were forced to accept that speed alone was no longer sufficient to protect a submarine. Production of Alfa has now ceased.

Cruise missile submarines

The attack submarine relies primarily upon antisubmarine and antiship torpedoes, but is also capable of deploying mines and, in some instances, land-attack cruise missiles such as the newly developed SS-NX-21. Similar in many respects to the US Tomahawk missile, the SS-NX-21 is small enough to be fired from a torpedo tube (possibly after modification), yet is capable of accurate delivery of a nuclear warhead at a distance of 1,950 miles (3,140 km). All Victor III, Yankee, Mike, Sierra and Akula-class SSNs can be converted to carry the SS-NX-21. If, in the future, war were to enter the nuclear stage, boats of the Mike and Victor III classes would use their new-technology pressurized hulls to full advantage, lying deep off the United States East Coast, ready to strike at targets inland.

Cruise missile submarines were developed in the 1950s for strategic attack and to counter US carrier task forces. At that

time, carriers had none of the long-range protection now provided by ASW aircrafts, such as the Viking, and they were vulnerable to long-range attack. Today, however, it is the cruise missile submarine that is highly vulnerable. The older submarines have to surface before they can fire the missile, and so give away their position. But they must also remain surfaced to feed mid-flight data to the missile, making them a target for enemy ASW shipping.

The Charlie- and Oscar-class SSGNs

The Charlie I-class SSGN, which entered service in 1968, was the first cruise missile submarine capable of firing while submerged. Fitted with eight antishipping cruise missiles, each with a range of 30 miles (50 km), Charlie I was later supplemented by Charlie II. This class was some 29½ feet (9 m) longer, faster, and armed with the SS-N-9 with an enhanced range of 69 miles (111 km). Although now relatively old, Charlie Is and IIs still provide a potent antishipping platform.

The Oscar-class SSGNs, the first of which was launched at Severodvinsk in 1980, are the second largest submarines in the world, having a displacement as great as that of many conventional cruisers. Their principal weapon is the new SS-N-19, with 24 missiles housed in vertical tubes, mounted 12 each side of the long, low fin. With their extreme range of 227 miles (365 km), these missiles can be fired at the outer operational limits of the United States' Viking aircraft. Patrols by Oscar-class SSBNs became a regular feature in 1985 and more are being built. Until the United States finds a way of countering the threat they pose, its once impregnable carrier force is potentially at risk.

The development of deep-water submarines, capable of carrying nuclear-tipped missiles, that can destroy enemy land installations without surfacing and giving away their own position, was realized early by the Soviet Union. But first attempts to build a suitable submarine platform were dogged by mechanical problems. These were subsequently overcome and an energetic building program begun. In fact, today the Soviet ballistic missile fleet far outnumbers the combined fleets of the United States, United Kingdom and France. By the end of 1974, the Soviet Navy was operating 34 Yankee-class SSBNs, each armed with 16 nuclear-tipped missiles with a range of 2,000 miles (3,200 km).

The Delta-class SSBN

The most successful of all SSBNs is undoubtedly the Delta class. Delta I entered service in 1973. It displaced 11,000 tons submerged, had 12 tubes for SS-N-8 missiles, each with an estimated range of 5,000 miles (8,000 km), and was the largest submarine of its day. Delta IIs and IIIs are armed with 16 SS-N-8 and SS-N-18 missiles respectively and are some 50 feet (15 m) longer than Delta I. All missiles carried by Delta-class SSBNs have Multiple Independently-targeted Reentry Vehicles (MIRVs) carrying up to seven warheads per missile. All are capable of reaching targets in North America while remaining in home waters.

The Typhoon-class SSBN

The Typhoon-class SSBN, built in the Severodvinsk yards on the White Sea, entered service in 1980 and is now the largest submarine in the world. Armed with 20 SS-N-20 solid fuel

Left: The Soviet *Victor III*, first seen in 1968, is a nuclear-powered attack submarine armed with both anti-submarine missiles and torpedoes. Target detection is assisted by fin-mounted towed array sonar.

Above: Despite being noisier and easier to detect than their Western counterparts, and forced by the range of their missiles to launch close to the coast, the Yankee-class SSBNs will still cause an ASW problem for US forces.

SSBMs, each with between six and nine MIRVs, the Typhoon can launch a missile capable of threatening any part of the United States without first leaving the protection of its bases with the Northern Fleet.

Clearly the Soviets are continuing to develop all aspects of submarine warfare and are giving this development the highest priority. Many classes of submarine in service are less than five years old and the introduction of still later, improved variants is anticipated. The newer submarine classes are showing technological advances not seen elsewhere in the armed forces. Undoubtedly, the role played by Soviet submarines in Warsaw Pact offensive thinking will go on growing for many years to come.

NATO

Given the growth in the Warsaw Pact fleet, it is perhaps surprising that Nato does not operate any cruise missile submarines (SSGNs). Nor does it intend to do so in the near future. Until recently, the only NATO navies to operate nuclear-powered attack submarines were the United States Navy and Royal Navy. Now the French are building a class of small nuclear submarines for use both in the Mediterranean and Atlantic and already have two in service.

NATO SSNs are still technologically ahead of those of the Warsaw Pact and their builders show no inclination to surrender this lead. The United States is continuing to build new nuclear-powered attack submarines on a regular basis. In the UK HMS *Triumph*, when completed, will be the latest of the Trafalgar class, and the 19th nuclear submarine to enter Royal Navy service.

The Skipjack and Thresher SSNs

The earliest SSNs still in service are the five US Skipjacks. Small and fast, these submarines were commissioned between 1959 and 1961. Originally there was a sixth boat of this class, but tragically USS *Scorpion* was lost at sea in 1968. Powered by a then highly advanced Westinghouse SSW pressurized water-cooled reactor (PWR), and equipped with single-screw propulsion, the Skipjacks introduced many features that were retained in later submarine classes. Advanced sonar electronics were sacrificed in favor of lightness. The Skipjacks weighed only 3,513 tons submerged, and were capable of a speed of over 30 knots (56 km/h) submerged.

The later Thresher and Sturgeon classes were larger and carried four 21-inch torpedo tubes (Skipjack carried six) as well as the SUBROC nuclear-tipped antisubmarine missile with a range of 23-35 miles (37-56 km). To operate the new offensive weaponry, more advanced BQS-system passive, upward-looking and active radars were required. The powerplant was not, however, increased to compensate for the additional weight, resulting in a slight reduction in the top speed. Fourteen boats of the Thresher class were commissioned between 1962 and 1967. USS *Thresher* itself was lost at sea with its crew in 1963.

The Los Angeles attack-class submarine

Between 1967 and 1975, 37 boats of the highly successful Sturgeon class were commissioned and all are now in operational service. The latest, most powerful United States attack-class submarine is the Los Angeles class, the first of which entered service in 1976. By the time the last of them has been completed, the number commissioned will have reached a

Far left: The introduction of the SS-N-8 and the Delta-class submarines marked a significant advance in Soviet SLBM capability, further improved with the delivery of the SS-N-18 and Delta III, seen here.

Above: As the largest submarine in the world, the *Typhoon* may be easy to detect – but it can use its long range SS-N-20 missiles to seek the protection of home waters or the Arctic icecap.

Left: The Dutch Zwaardvis class is one of the largest types of conventional submarines currently in service. Armed with torpedoes, it can operate in the Atlantic with a top speed of 20 knots in support of NATO operations.

staggering 58! Much larger than their predecessors, these boats have a submerged weight of 6,900 tons and a top speed in excess of 30 knots. They are equipped with very long- range BQQ-5 sonar and the BQS-15 short-range system, supplemented by towed arrays, enabling them to track Warsaw Pact nuclear submarines under any conditions. They are, without doubt, the most sophisticated submarines of their kind in service in the world today. Weapon fits can include SUBROC, Harpoon and Tomahawk, as well as conventional and wire-guided torpedoes. The later Los Angeles-class submarines are fitted with 15 vertical launch tubes for the Tomahawk missiles. With such an array of weaponry, these submarines have an offensive capacity not only against other submarines, but also against long-range shipping targets and strategic shore-based targets far inland.

The tremendous sophistication of these boats poses a problem of cost. Whereas the first boat commissioned in 1976 was estimated at $221.25 million, by 1984 the cost had risen to $663 million. At this rate, the time will come when Washington will have to think twice about future construction and development.

Above: Not only does the USS *Groton*, a Los Angeles class of SSN, have an attack capability against surface vessels and submarines, but it can also lay mines or strike strategic targets with Tomahawk cruise missiles.

Right: The latest in British nuclear-powered attack submarines, HMS *Turbulent* is one of the Trafalgar class of SSNs that will spearhead the hunt for Soviet SSBNs as they break through into the Atlantic or hide in home waters.

UK submarines

The first British submarine, HMS *Dreadnought,* had an American Skipjack propulsion plant, but the later Valiant and Trafalgar classes are of all-British design. All British boats are armed with 21-inch torpedo tubes and have no equivalent of SUBROC. Lately, however, the British government has ordered the new Stingray torpedo, reputed to be the only lightweight torpedo capable of penetrating the pressurized hulls of any Warsaw Pact submarine. Most certainly, Royal Navy SSBNs will be equipped with these when they are available. It is also likely that Harpoon will soon be fitted, giving British boats excellent capabilities against not only Warsaw Pact submarines, but also surface vessels up to a range of 57 miles (92 km).

Like the United States, the United Kingdom is also experiencing problems in funding new technology. HMS *Swiftsure* was built in 1981 at a cost of £37.1 million. The estimated cost of HMS *Triumph,* ordered in January 1986, is in excess of £200 million.

Diesel submarines

Currently NATO has about 170 conventional diesel submarines operational or on order. Of these, all but five are operated by European members or Canada. The United States has now relegated its last remaining conventional submarines to secondary duties in the Pacific. Diesel submarines fall into three distinct categories, reflecting the different needs of their operators. Large ocean-going submarines are held by those nations with a North Atlantic role, coastal submarines are in service with countries responsible exclusively for their own defense, while medium-sized boats are operated by all of the principal Mediterranean powers.

The foremost ocean-going diesel submarines are the Oberon and Porpoise classes operated by the United Kingdom and Canada. At present, four Porpoise-class submarines, built between 1954 and 1958, are in service with the Royal Navy while 13 Oberons, built between 1957 and 1964, operate with the Royal Navy, and three with the Canadians. These boats operate on batteries in almost complete silence, making them very difficult to detect while submerged, and their past record on NATO exercises has been excellent. They are, however, based on technology of the 1950s and are now dangerously out of date.

The UK Upholder-class

Britain has accepted that there will be an operational need for conventionally powered submarines for several years to come and is now building the Upholder-class, which will be in service for the rest of this century. Originally, it was planned to build a total of 10 Upholders, at the rate of one per year. But in January 1986, a bulk order for three boats was placed, and the rate of production will now almost certainly be accelerated. With newly designed engine mountings to reduce radiated noise to a minimum, the Upholder will be one of the most silent submarines operational anywhere in the world. It will be equipped with six torpedo tubes and will be capable of operating either conventional or Stingray torpedoes, Harpoon missiles or mines.

The Dutch Zwaardvis and Walrus submarines

As part of their overall NATO commitment, the Dutch have

HMS *Revenge* sails through the waters of the Clyde in Scotland where the British SSBN's are based. At least one of the boats can be kept at sea at all times as Britain's independent nuclear deterrent.

undertaken to supply North Atlantic task forces and are presently completing the last of a class of six Zwaardvis submarines. These are armed with six 21-inch torpedo tubes and equipped with the latest automated fire control and command systems, giving them an offensive capability similar to that of the British Oberons. The Dutch intend to replace their old Dolphins, built in the 1950s, with six new Walrus-class submarines to be built in the late 1980s and early 1990s. Walruses will carry all the technology of firepower of the British Upholders and will provide excellent additional cover in the open spaces of the Greenland-Iceland-United Kingdom (GIUK) Gap.

NATO coastal support

The vast majority of coastal submarines are West German in design. West Germany itself operates 24 such boats in two Baltic-based squadrons. In such confined waters, their lifespan would be short, but they would be able to inflict heavy losses on the Soviet Baltic fleet and could play a crucial role in frustrating attempts by the Warsaw Pact to land amphibious forces in Denmark or northern Germany. Denmark operates two modern modified Type-205 coastal submarines, and Norway a further 15. These would be used exclusively for coastal defense, but their presence could play a useful role in the defeat of the Warsaw Pact in the Norwegian Sea.

France sees her responsibilities as divided between the Atlantic and the Mediterranean. Until recently, she operated six ocean-going Naval-class boats in the Atlantic but has now replaced two of these with the first of her nuclear-powered boats. Four Agosta and seven Daphne-class submarines are stationed in the Mediterranean and would be used in support of the US carrier task force in time of war. Whereas the old Daphne-class boats are small and accident-prone, the Agostas are large, silent and capable of firing their torpedoes from the seabed.

Submarine nuclear deterrence

Submarine nuclear deterrence within NATO is provided by the USA, UK and France. The US Benjamin Franklin and Lafayette classes, of which there are altogether 31, form the backbone of the SSBN fleets. They were built between 1961 and 1966 to

Above: The *Woodrow Wilson*, a Lafayette class SSBN of the US Navy carries 16 Poseidon missiles, as well as torpedoes and the anti-submarine missile Subroc, at a submerged speed of up to 30 knots.

Below: The *Narhvalen*, a type 205 submarine of the Danish Navy, is towed out to sea. Based on the expertise gained in World War II, this class was designed as a small coastal boat in Germany in the 1950s. It also serves with the German and Norwegian navies.

take the Polaris missile, and were subsequently converted to take the C-3 Poseidon SLBM. Twelve are now undergoing a further conversion to fit the C-4 Trident missile. The Ohio-class, which was purpose-built to carry 26 Trident missiles, has a submerged weight of 18,700 tons – twice the size of any other NATO submarine. The United States is well aware that the Soviet Union now has the potential to bombard it with missiles fired from submarines submerged in the Baltic and White Seas, and has developed the Trident missile as a means of retaliation. When the full complement of 24 Ohio-class submarines is completed, the Americans will be more than able to match the Soviets in this field.

Britain and Trident

The United Kingdom operates four Resolution-class submarines. Although these boats are purely British in design, the Polaris missiles that they carry were purchased direct from the United States. Modernization plans have been put into effect to keep this small fleet up to date until the late 1990s, when it is intended to replace them with a new class of SSBNs capable of firing the Trident II missile. Scarcely has any defense-procurement program within the United Kingdom aroused as much controversy as that surrounding Trident, and it is quite likely that a future Labour government would scrap this program.

The French Le Redoutable-class SSBNs

France's maritime nuclear deterrent is produced entirely from its own national resources. The five SSBNs of the Le Redoutable class became operational between 1971 and 1980. *L'Inflexible,* with improved propulsion and electronics, entered service in 1985 and a seventh boat is presently under construction. It is intended to replace the five first-generation boats with a completely new class between 1990 and 2000. Unlike certain elements within the UK, France has absolutely no intention of scrapping its maritime nuclear deterrent (*"force de frappe"*), either now or in the future.

Over twice as big as the Lafayette class, the USS *Ohio* is the first of its class of SSBNs, seen here alongside a dock with crew members on deck and a gantry carrying power cables.

COMPARISON OF WARSAW PACT AND NATO ATTACK SUBMARINES

Class	Nationality	Armament	Propulsion	Submerged Displacement (tons)	Entry into Service
Tango (SS)	USSR	Torpedoes ASW missiles	Diesel	3,800	1973
Charlie II (SSGN)	USSR	Torpedoes SS-N-9 antiship cruise missile	Nuclear	5,300	1974
Victor III (SSN)	USSR	Torpedoes SS-N-16 ASW missile	Nuclear	6,200	1979
Alfa (SSN)	USSR	Torpedoes SS-N-15 ASW missile	Nuclear	3,600	1978
Oscar (SSGN)	USSR	Torpedoes SS-N-19 antiship cruise missile	Nuclear	13,800	1981
Kilo (SS)	USSR	Torpedoes	Diesel	2,900	1980
Mike (SSN)	USSR	Torpedoes ASW missile	Nuclear	9,500	1983
Sierra (SSN)	USSR	Torpedoes ASW missile	Nuclear	8,000	1984
Yankee (SSN)	USSR	Torpedoes land-attack cruise missile	Nuclear	12,800	1984
Akula (SSN)	USSR	Torpedoes ASW missile	Nuclear	7,800	1985
Los Angeles (SSN)	USA	Torpedoes harpoon antiship tomahawk SLCM SUBROC ASW rocket	Nuclear	6,400	1976
Sturgeon (SSN)	USA	Harpoon antiship SUBROC ASW rocket	Nuclear	4,600	1967
Swiftsure (SSN)	UK	Tigerfish torpedoes	Nuclear	4,500	1978

SS: Diesel SSN: Nuclear SSGN: Nuclear-cruise

While the United States controls the vast majority of the maritime nuclear deterrent, the potential roles to be played by British and French submarines in any future war would be crucial. Between them, Britain and France can maintain four or five SSBNs at sea at any one time. Should the Soviet Union ever attempt to fight a war confined to Europe, in the hope that the United States would hold back, these boats alone could inflict appreciable damage on Russian cities. The Soviet Union would thus be denied the possibility of limited warfare.

Escort Vessels

Warsaw Pact

All major surface units in Warsaw Pact service are Soviet except for one Katlin-class destroyer, in service with the Polish navy. Many destroyers are old, hampered by short-range weaponry,

Above: Aerial view of a Krivak I frigate. The bulky quadruple launcher for the SS-N-14 antisubmarine missile is clearly visible forward, with the two 76-mm turrets to the rear. The cream-colored circles are the pop-up SA-N-4 SAM system.

Top: The East German frigate *Rostock*, one of the Soviet Koni class, is the largest ship that would be available to the Warsaw Pact's maritime operations in the Baltic.

and ill-suited to the specialist roles forced upon them.

The Koshia- and Kanin-class destroyers

The Koshia-class destroyers, the first of which was built in 1962, were the first series-built warships in the world to rely exclusively upon gas-turbine power. They were designed to give AAW and ASW protection to the Kynda-class cruisers, each Kynda operating with a flotilla of three or four Koshias. Since 1974, many of this class have undergone modernization and now mount four 30-mm air-defense guns and four short-range SS-N-2 launchers, as well as variable-depth sonars. Even after their conversion, the 19 Koshias in service still suffer from low performance and are relegated to general-purpose roles when not assigned to cruiser escort.

The Kanin-class guided missile destroyer, of which eight are in service with the Baltic and Northern Fleets, are successful conversions of Krupny-class ships that are now obsolete. Each Kanin is armed with eight 57-mm guns in quadruple mounts and eight 30-mm antiaircraft guns in twin mounts. Two quintuple torpedo tubes and a twin SA-N-1 launcher are fitted for close-encounter ASW work. The ships also carry a relatively antiquated sonar, which very probably would not prove effective in detecting the new classes of small diesel submarines operated by NATO in those waters.

The Krivak-class guided-missile destroyers

The Krivak-class guided missile destroyers are potentially the most lethal ships of their type in the Soviet navy. They are comparatively small as well as cheap and easy to build. Construction takes place in the small shipyards of the Baltic and Black Seas, leaving the more traditional White Sea yards free for the building of larger units. The major ASW system fitted is the SS-N-14 missile, mounted forward in a bulky quadruple container. This is supplemented by RBU 6000 mortars and torpedo tubes. Air defense is notably lacking. Short range SA-N-4 "bins" are located fore and aft, and newer ships (designated Krivak IIs) have a single 100-mm gun, but there are no "last ditch" missile systems. Evidently, the Krivak class was not designed to withstand air attacks unaided, or operate in deep seas. There are more than 40 of this class, and they would probably be found in large ASW flotillas operating in home waters under the protection of Soviet land-based air cover.

A Royal Navy Amazon-class Type 21, typical of modern general-purpose frigates, turning at speed in the North Atlantic. These ships are armed with a 4.5-inch gun, Exocet SSM, Seacat SAM and torpedoes and carry a Lynx ASW helicopter.

NATO

NATO escort ships not only outnumber those of the Warsaw Pact, they also outclass them. But that does not mean that NATO superiority in the escort role is assured. Whereas Warsaw Pact escort ships would hardly ever be asked to leave home waters and would always operate in conjunction with land-based aircraft, NATO escorts must be able to fulfill a number of totally different roles. These include patrolling home waters, protecting merchant convoys that cross the North Atlantic, operating as scouts for US carrier task forces, and participating in submarine-hunting battle groups based on British ASW carriers. To carry out all of these tasks, NATO would need four times as many support ships as it has already. For instance, NATO would require 500 shiploads to ferry reinforcements from Britain to Continental Europe in the first month of a war, and a further 1,000 shiploads to carry US reinforcements across the North Atlantic. Thereafter, 500 ships per month would need to cross from the United States to various parts of Europe to carry the minimum supplies required.

The average merchant ship is capable of speeds of more than 20 knots (40 km/h), not much slower than escorting warships. Very probably, future convoys would sail so fast that if, for any reason, the escort ships were detached from the convoy, they would not be able to regain contact. While not all Soviet submarines carry torpedoes, most certainly at the start of any conflict there would be several cruise missile boats at sea, each capable of threatening a convoy from beyond the range of the escorts' sonar. NATO monitors Soviet submarine movements carefully and would be suspicious if an unusually large number of boats were to put to sea simultaneously. To launch a surprise attack, most of the Warsaw Pact submarines would have to start from their home bases and negotiate the Greenland-Iceland-United Kingdom (GIUK) Gap on the way to their battle stations. NATO has sown this vulnerable area with passive sound-seeking sonars such as SOSUS. Very likely, most enemy craft seeking passage through these waters would be located. It would then be the task of ASW escorts to pinpoint any enemy submarine and destroy it.

The US Spruance-class destroyers

Different members of NATO have developed their own escort

vessels according to their military requirements. The US Navy operates two types of escort. The larger types, designed to act as carrier task force escorts, are fast, well-armed and expensive, whereas the convoy escorts are smaller, slower and far cheaper to build. Among the most successful of the carrier escorts are the Spruance-class destroyers. At 7,810 tons fully laden, the Spruances are twice the size of their predecessors. Their large hulls and block superstructures can carry huge stores of the latest, high-technology hardware, which can easily be updated by modular replacement in due course. In essence, the cost of the boat (the "platform") has been minimized to enable maximum expenditure to go on weaponry ("payload"). The ASW equipment carried is formidable. The ASROC launcher, with its magazine carrying 24 reloads (three times as much as Soviet escorts) is supported by two triple torpedo tubes and two LAMPS III helicopters. It also carries two quadruple Harpoon missiles, an octuple Sea Sparrow launcher, two 5-inch (127-mm) guns and two Phalanx CIWS. Thirty-two ships of this class are in service around the world and, in time of war, would continue to operate in close cooperation with the 12 carriers.

The Oliver Hazard Perry class of frigate epitomizes the low-cost patrol vessel now in US service in large numbers. The single-screw engine is economical and easy to maintain. Construction of the entire ship has been made as simple as possible to enable it to be built in small yards. Armed with a single Harpoon launcher, a 3-inch gun and a Phalanx CIWS, the 52 ships of this class are designed to provide escort protection

Below: Designed to provide air defense for a task force, this Type 42 destroyer, HMS *Manchester*, is equipped with the Sea Dart missile system capable of intercepting high- or low-flying aircraft or missiles, or being used against surface targets.

Left: The USS *Spruance* was lead ship in a class that was primarily tasked with antisubmarine warfare including operations as a carrier escort. These ships are now undergoing modernization to keep them effective into the next century.

for the present, rather than future. Any major refit involving the addition of new equipment would prove difficult.

British escorts

British escorts are also divided between those with advanced air-defense systems and those specializing in ASW. One of the Royal Navy's key roles in time of war will be the patrolling of the GIUK Gap, and many of its new destroyers are specially designed for this purpose. During the Falklands War, the British Royal Navy was shown to be very vulnerable to long-range missile attack from the air. Consequently Type 22 (Broadsword class) destroyers have been equipped with Sea Wolf as a localized AAW defense. Sea Wolf is also being fitted to the new Type 23 class presently under construction. The older ships, however, will rely on the umbrella of NATO air cover for their survival.

France, Canada and the Netherlands all operate destroyers capable of North Atlantic operations. In contrast, the majority of the Dutch, Belgian and German fleets are coastal and would thus concentrate on defending channel convoys.

Below: The Standing Naval Force Atlantic (STANAVFORLANT) consists of destroyer-class frigates from the NATO navies that work as a multinational team. Here, eight vessels are led by a British Type-22 destroyer.

Right: HMCS *Protecteur*, a Canadian replenishment ship, prepares to refuel HMCS *Annapolis*, while supplying a DDH 280-class destroyer. The frigate's ASW helicopter, a Sea King, hovers to their stern.

509

Air Power

Manned Bombers

Warsaw Pact

As well as holding and renewing huge stockpiles of strategic missiles, both superpowers know the potential impact of the manned bomber and maintain these forces accordingly. The Warsaw Pact now operates a fleet containing over 800 operational aircraft; of these, 450 are elderly Tu-16 Badgers no longer in production, 115 are Tu-95 Bear variants now back in limited production, 140 are Tu-22 Blinders and a further 130 are Tu-26 Backfires. A revolutionary swing-wing jet, codenamed Blackjack, has now been trialled and is expected to enter service in 1987.

Below: Like the Badger, Tupolev Tu-95 and 142 Bears perform a variety of roles, regularly encountering NATO air-defense patrols. Here a tail gunner in a Bear comes face to face with pilots of a USAF F-4 Phantom.

Armed with bombs or weapons such as the AS-15 cruise missile, Blackjack will be the first effective strategic bomber that can carry out missions into US airspace, combining both the range and speed that earlier Bears did not possess.

All Soviet aircraft are capable of striking at any part of European NATO. It is estimated that the Long Range Air Force could drop 1,200 tons of explosive per day anywhere in Europe. This is four times the amount dropped on England by the Luftwaffe in the worst 24 hours of the Blitz, and could obviously include not only conventional but also nuclear bombs.

At the time of the SALT II negotiations, the Soviets argued successfully that because the Tu-26 could not fly non-stop across the North Atlantic and back, it should not be regarded as a strategic bomber. But since then most models have been retrofitted with in-flight refuelling probes, and a number of elderly Tu-16 Badgers converted to tanker duties.

It is likely that both the new Blackjack and the latest Bear H variant will be armed with the new subsonic AS-15 cruise missile. Earlier Bears are also being upgraded to Bear G standard, replacing the old subsonic AS-3 Kangaroo air-to-surface missile with the far superior supersonic AS-4. A manned bomber attack by aircraft firing stand-off missiles against the mainland United States would be very costly – but it can no longer be regarded as impossible. It is certain that at least a few aircraft would be successful in evading US outer defenses, particularly as US air defenses have been steadily eroded over the last decade.

The Bear bomber

The Bear bomber has been the traditional workhorse of Soviet Long Range Aviation. With a range of 7,800 miles (12,500 km) – or further still when fitted with an in-flight refuelling probe – the original models first introduced in 1956 were capable of carrying 25,000 lbs (11,250 kg) of conventional or nuclear free-fall bombs. Powered by four relatively old-technology Kuznetsov NK-12MV turboprop engines, the huge eight-blade contra-rotating propellers are still highly efficient – allowing a top speed of 540 mph (860 km/h), the equivalent of many modern civilian jet aircraft. Six NR-23 23-mm cannon are normally fitted for defense, two in a manned tail turret and two in remotely controlled dorsal and ventral turrets. The Bear B, with its large nose radar, was first fitted operationally with the AS-3 Kangaroo air-to-surface missile as long ago as 1963. These older models are now being retrofitted with the AS-4 Kitchen which has a range of 286 miles (460 km) on high-altitude profile, and is equipped with a warhead of 350 kiloton (nuclear) and 2,200 lbs/990 kg (conventional) with a speed of Mach 3.5.

Backfire

The first TU-26 Backfire was developed in 1964 with the first model designated Backfire A, flying operationally in 1969. Few aircraft have since been the subject of so much speculation and controversy. The initial Backfire A suffered from a considerable range deficiency due to excessive drag, but with the introduction of the much modified Backfire B in 1975 (with its considerably increased outer wingspan, distinctive double-tapered trailing edge and new inward-retracting landing gear), this problem has been overcome. And the range of certain models has been considerably enhanced by the introduction of in-flight refuelling pods. Powered by two 45,000-lb (20,250-kg) Kuznetsov NK-144 afterburning turbofan engines, Backfire has a maximum speed of approximately 1,300 mph (2,000 km/h) at 36,000 ft (10,800 m). Armed with the AS-4 Kitchen or AS-6 Kingfish missiles (the latter has a maximum range of 350 miles/560 km at Mach 3), an alternative load of 17,500 lbs (7,800 kg) of nuclear or conventional free-fall bombs may be carried.

Blackjack

Existence of the Tupolev Blackjack has been rumored since the late 1970s and, via the unusual medium of a politically-accepted leak, a satellite image printout has been available since 1981. Production is now taking place at the gigantic Kazan State Aviation Factory, and it is likely that the first production models will appear late in 1986. Little is known about this aircraft in the West. Vastly differing statistics have been published – but what is certain is that Blackjack is of a revolutionary new design. It is thought possible that four Backfire engines have been fitted, but this is not certain; if Blackjack is to cross the North Atlantic and back, it will require so great a fuel capacity that the bomb load will have to be reduced to 36,000 lbs (16,200 kg). However, it is also likely that Blackjack will be armed with the new AS-15 missile, and may incorporate stealth technology similar to that of the US Rockwell B-1B – but details are still far from complete.

What is certain is that the Soviet Union has totally reversed its early policy of running down its bomber fleet. New aircraft are being designed and built and existing models updated. Cruise missiles, so heavily criticized by the Soviet Union when deployed by NATO, are now carried by many bombers and are constantly being renewed. Soviet Long Range Aviation must no longer be regarded as a past strength, but as a future threat.

NATO

Long-range manned bombers are still an integral part of the strategic armories of American and French air forces. Equipped with the most up-to-date electronics to prevent the aircraft's

Left: The Tupolev Tu-16 Badger first flew in 1952 and is still operational in a number of variants. These include strategic and antishipping bombers armed with both conventional and nuclear weapons, and maritime and electronic reconnaissance.

Below: The Tupolev Tu-22M, Backfire, which entered service in the 1970s is capable of reaching any part of Europe and much of the Atlantic. It can be armed with missiles such as this AS-4 Kitchen, with its own range of nearly 300 miles (500 km).

location and identification for as long a time as possible, these aircraft will try and penetrate the highly complex belts of Warsaw Pact surface-to-air missiles, getting a substantial minority far enough through the defenses to launch stand-off missiles, or drop nuclear or conventional gravity bombs. It was originally planned to deploy 3,000 Boeing AGM-86B Air-Launched Cruise Missiles (ALCMs), to be carried by these aircraft by the 1990s – but this number has now been reduced to 1,500. Fourteen USAF Wings operate a total of 167 B-52G and 96 B-52H bombers; at present two Wings of FB-111As are in service and will remain so until the introduction of the Northrop Advanced Technology (Stealth) bomber, when they will be reassigned to Tactical Air Command.

After a checkered early career, the first Rockwell B-1B bomber flew three months ahead of schedule (at below contract price!), and it is now anticipated that all 100 aircraft on order should be operational by early 1988. Twenty-nine B-1B bombers have operated from Dyess Air Force Base, Texas, since June 1985 and are now entering service at bases in Ellsworth, South Carolina and McConnell, Kansas. The B-1B bomber will be used in a deep penetration mode until the introduction of the Stealth

Above: Originally designed in the late 1940s, Boeing's B-52 has undergone constant modification to retain its place as a bomber and missile platform for both conventional and nuclear weapons. It will probably remain in service into the next century.

Below: A Boeing B-52G refuels from a KC-135 tanker. Clearly visible are the two underwing pylons, carrying AGM-86B cruise missiles. The internal bomb-bay also holds a variety of missiles and other weapons.

The USAF's Lockheed SR-71 Blackbird is a strategic reconnaissance aircraft relying on speed and altitude for protection. Capable of long range, it can cover large amounts of territory and has probably witnessed most trouble spots since the 1960s.

Since its conception in the 1960s, the Rockwell B-1 has had a checkered and controversial life. Though much better at penetrating enemy airspace than the B-52, it will never be available in sufficient numbers to replace it.

bomber, expected for 1992, when it will revert to a stand-off cruise missile carrier.

The B-52

The B-52 Stratofortress is an historical anomaly. Although it seems totally antiquated and vulnerable, over one billion dollars have been spent on the B-52 during the last 20 years to ensure its effectiveness into the 1990s. The prototype B-52 flew as long ago as April 1952, since which time 744 aircraft have been built and numerous alterations and improvements made. The B-52G, presently in service, was planned initially to be the final variant before the introduction of the completely new B-70 bomber. Structural alterations included the remoting of the quadruple 0.5-inch tail gun and repositioning the gunner's position in the fuselage center. Provision was also made for launching ECM decoys and, for the first time, stand-off missiles. When it became obvious that the B-70 project was to be cancelled, yet another variant – the B-52H – was developed. Powered by eight new Pratt & Whitney TF33 turbofan engines, and armed with a new 20-mm single General Electric Gatling gun, it was initially intended that the B-52H would carry the Skybolt ballistic missile. Skybolt was subsequently cancelled with the result that both the B-52G and H now carry either 20 SRAM (short-range attack missiles) or the new Boeing AGM-86B ALCM.

The B-1B

The B-1B bomber eventually entered service in 1986 after a staggering development period of 23 years, and outright cancellation by President Carter in 1977. Production of four aircraft per month is anticipated, with completion of the 100th late in 1988. During low-level penetration, at speeds of up to 600 mph (960 km/h), the wings will be partly or wholly swept and the radar cross-section reduced to a staggering one per cent of that of the B-52. A very costly defensive electronics system (designed by Eaton AIL Division) is fitted, as is a Boeing offensive electronics system designed to keep to a minimum unavoidable emissions, such as those from the radar altimeter, doppler and terrain-following radar. The weapons bay, which was originally built to carry the AGM-69 SRAM, was 14 ft (4.2 m) long, but subsequent (and not totally satisfactory) modifications have had to be made to enable it to accept the 20 ft 9 inch (6.27 m)-long AGM-86. In all, mixed loads of up to 76,000 lbs (34,200 kg) can be carried. However, this limitation is one of volume rather than weight; external pods for reducing the maximum speed and increasing dangerously the radar cross-section would have to be employed to carry such a load.

Little is known about the Advanced Technology Bomber (ATB), save that Northrop have been awarded a contract worth nearly $8 billion to develop it. The ATB will almost certainly be smaller than the B1-B but larger than the F-111B. Its radar cross-section is unlikely to be far superior to that of the B1-B and the top speed roughly similar.

France has a strategic bomber capability consisting of 33 Mirage IV aircraft in two wings. Armed either with AN-22 gravity bombs or a 60-70 kt nuclear warhead, these aircraft are tasked with low-level penetration, but are not deemed to have a potentially high success rate.

One of the greatest dangers to NATO manned bombers is their destruction on the ground as a result of a preemptive strike. It is hoped that new radar techniques have now alleviated this problem to a degree; indeed, one of the B1-B bomber's greatest assets is its ability to become airborne quickly. Although manned NATO bombers would have to face highly advanced Warsaw Pact defenses in any future war, their very existence has the effect of forcing the Soviets to expend huge resources to counter them. Clearly, the manned bomber will have a place in the NATO armory until at least the early part of the 21st century.

Strike Aircraft

Warsaw Pact

The Soviet Union alone is capable of fielding over 1,500 strike aircraft simultaneously. Up to 1,000 aircraft would almost certainly be tasked to pound defensive positions in the NATO front line during the first few hours of hostilities. The remaining aircraft, supported by long-range aviation bombers, would thereafter exploit any weaknesses created.

Subsequent short-range targets would include NATO airfields, command and control centers, signals concentrations and nuclear sites. Long-range sorties would therefore inevitably be left to the bomber fleets. Protection would be afforded by fighter escorts, probably MiG-21s or MiG-23s, with new generations of fighters now entering service, and by ECM carried in AN-12 and Tu-16 jamming aircraft. All aircraft are

Left: The Dassault-Breguet Mirage IV launching the ASMP nuclear stand-off missile, with both strategic and tactical roles. Air-delivered nuclear bombs or missiles form an important part of the French independent strategic policy.

Below: A development of the Su-7, with semivariable-geometry wings, the Sukhoi Su-17 Fitter is a ground-attack aircraft in service with both the Soviet and the Polish air forces.

equipped with terrain-avoidance radar and possibly terrain-following radar.

It is difficult to equate Warsaw Pact and NATO aircraft; the latter are fewer in number, but more sophisticated. It is anticipated that the Soviet Union would lose up to 15 per cent of its strike force during the first 24 hours of hostilities, and even if air superiority had by then been gained, they would not be able to launch so large a simultaneous attack again. It seems more likely that frontal aviation sorties would then be directed towards support of the army. Whereas NATO army officers are trained to initiate and direct small air strikes, this luxury is denied their Warsaw Pact equivalents, who must clear air strike requests at a high level before they are sanctioned. Therefore it is quite likely that Soviet air response would be on too large a scale and probably too late. The Soviets do, however, have sufficient aircraft to cruise over the battlefield seeking targets of opportunity.

With one highly important exception, Warsaw Pact strike aircraft have evolved from the Design Bureau of Pavel O. Sukhoi. The Su-7 Fitter first entered Soviet service in 1959, providing the Soviet Union with its basic fighter of the 1960s. Still on active service with Czechoslovakia, Hungary, Poland and Romania, this useful and sturdy aircraft is capable of operating

Top: An artist's impression showing the Sukhoi Su-25 Frogfoot over mountainous terrain. A close-support aircraft with a long loiter time, large payload and internally mounted gun, Frogfoot has been used extensively in Afghanistan.

Above: The Sukhoi Su-24 Fencer is capable of striking deep into NATO territory, protected by its high speed and comprehensive EW/ECM fit. It has a range of 200 miles (320 km) fully loaded with 17,600 lbs (8,000 kg) or of over 1,000 miles (1,600 km) carrying a third of that weight.

from rough airfields. It does, however, suffer from a very short range (the result of a large engine and small fuel tank) so that external fuel tanks must be carried at the expense of an already limited payload, on any but the shortest of missions.

The Su-17 Fitter

Much improved in design and powered by the advanced AL-21F engine, the Su-17 Fitter C first entered service in 1971 and immediately assumed the mantle of senior Soviet strike aircraft. Capable of speeds of Mach 1.1, the Su-17 was far superior to the Su-7 in all respects. A total of 8,820 lbs (3,970 kg) of ordnance or extra fuel can be carried on eight hardpoints mounted in tandem pairs under the fuselage and wings. The SRD-5M "high fix" radar carried within the center body is fitted to Soviet aircraft, but not to the export variant (designated Su-20) which is in operation with the Polish Air Force. The Su-20 has only two ventral pylons, enabling it to carry four extra fuel tanks, and it must be assumed that the Poles would utilize the aircraft in a long-range strike role. The majority of the Su-17s currently in Soviet service are of the Fitter D variant which first entered

The McDonnell-Douglas Harrier, shown here, was developed from the British Harrier to meet the US Marine Corps requirement for a "bomb truck" to give close support to ground troops. It is capable of carrying 17,000 lbs (7,700 kg) of munitions when using a short take-off.

service in 1977, and is still in limited production. The pilot's view is facilitated by a lengthened and downward-sloped nose, whilst a combination of a laser ranger and marked-target seeker, a terrain-following radar and doppler, combine to make Fitter D a very formidable adversary.

The Su-24 Fencer

The Su-24 Fencer was originally designated a fighter aircraft by NATO but is actually an attack and interdiction aircraft. Capable of long-range, all-weather performance, the Su-24 Fencer (over 450 are in Soviet service) was much influenced in design by the General Dynamics F-111 and the Panavia Tornado. Capable of making blind pin-point strikes, the aerodynamics are an advanced variant of those proven in the MiG-23 series. The pilot and navigator sit side by side in fairly cramped conditions behind a powerful pulse-doppler radar. Basic inertial radar is supplemented by terrain and forward-looking attack radars, laser and ECM/EW electronics. The Su-24 is not so much a "deep interdiction" aircraft as an all-weather, large payload platform back-up for the MiG-27. The range of the Su-24, particularly at high altitudes, enables the aircraft to be based in the relatively safe western Soviet Union, rather than in the more vulnerable satellite nations. Utilizing its "hi-lo-hi" profile, Su-24 can reach every major NATO air base in continental Europe and most of them in eastern Britain.

The MiG-27

The most advanced aircraft in the Soviet strike fleet is the highly advanced MiG-27 Flogger D, of which over 500 are presently in service. Based on the MiG-23 multirole fighter, MiG-27 contains many specialist developments not found in the faster and more versatile original. A vast array of electronics, as yet unidentified, are housed in the downward-sloping nose. Air-to-air ranging equipment, used in conjunction with the newly-developed 23-mm rotary cannon, is fitted in the small radome at the tip of the nose above a doppler navigation radar system. CW target-illuminating radars are carried to the rear of the nose, and SRO-2M "odd rods" Identification Friend or Foe (IFF) and forward-looking "swift-rod" line scan are also carried. Pilot visibility, originally a problem with the MiG-23 series, has been much improved by the installation of a higher level cockpit with its deeper hinged hood and windshield. The main tyres are fatter than usual to ease the landing of this heavy aircraft on rough landing strips, while auxiliary rocket-assisted take-off (RATO) units are fitted to rear fuselage racks to reduce take-off very effectively to 2,625 ft (788 m). Although the quoted weapon load is relatively low, the

Top left: Not strictly a strike aircraft, the Czechoslovak L-39 Albatross is employed as a basic jet trainer in the Warsaw Pact. Its ability to carry weapons is limited, apart from the gun mounted in a pod under the fuselage.

Above: This Tornado GR 1 of the RAF carries a load of long-range tanks, ECM pods, Sidewinder missiles and two Hunting JP 233 airfield Attack Weapon Systems, which dispense a mixture of runway-cratering munitions and area-denial mines.

Left: Still serving with the US Air Force and Navy the Vought A-7 Corsair II has been bought by both Greece and Portugal as a cost effective strike aircraft with improvements to engine and avionics and capable of carrying 15,000 lbs of weapons as well as an internal 20-mm cannon.

A ground crewman performs maintenance on a Fairchild A-10 Thunderbolt II, the only dedicated close-support attack aircraft of its type in NATO. Thunderbolt is armed with a massive 30-mm cannon and can carry 16,000 lbs (7,200 kg) of ordnance mounted on 11 pylons.

MiG-27 is capable of carrying the latest tactical missiles, together with fuel/air explosives, cluster and laser-guided "smart" bombs.

The Su-25 Frogfoot

Perhaps the most interesting aircraft to enter Soviet service recently has been the Su-25 Frogfoot "tank-killer". One hundred are now operational; first seen in the skies of Afghanistan in 1982, the Su-25 first entered service before trials were fully completed. Intended to rival the United States' Fairchild A-10, but closer in design to the less successful Northrop A-9, Frogfoot has an unswept, high-aspect-ratio wing set high on the fuselage. The rear fuselage resembles the F4 Phantom, with its single fin and horizontal tail mounted on a fuselage extension. Cockpit visibility is good forward and downward, but somewhat restricted to the rear. The tried and tested MiG-21 Turmansky engines give adequate, if subsonic performance, although bombing in Afghanistan has always been carried out at high altitude with little apparent accuracy. It may well be that if the Su-25 Frogfoot were ever used in the European theater it would supplement the Hind D & E helicopters in an antihelicopter role, leaving the destruction of NATO armor to the extensive army resources.

NATO

NATO is fully aware that in any future conflict with the Warsaw Pact, the role of its strike aircraft would be to slow down the enemy's advance forces as far as possible whilst disrupting its second and third echelons – thus giving the ground forces time to reform, and if possible, to counter-attack. But, beyond this initial principle, NATO shows little unity. The USAF, with the lessons of Vietnam in mind, regards air superiority and the suppression of Warsaw Pact SAM sites as paramount, whilst European NATO regards this as an unrealistic drain on resources. While the USAF practices the execution of high-altitude, deep-thrust missions, western European air forces concentrate on fast low-level air strikes often executed at heights as low as 100 ft (30 m).

The A-10

Few aircraft epitomize this diversity of aims more than the Fairchild Republic A-10A Thunderbolt. Capable of operating from short, unprepared airstrips, the A-10 is armed with an immensely powerful 30-mm seven-barrel Gatling gun capable of firing a staggering 2,100 or 4,200 rounds per minute; it is also capable of carrying up to 16,000 lbs (7,200 kg) of mixed munitions, stowed externally on eleven pylons. The two General Electric TF34-100 turbofan engines are so designed that the pilot, seated in a titanium "bath-tub" for protection, can retain control with one engine completely shot away.

Although ideally suited for ultra-low-level antitank attack, the USAF pilots concentrate their training on high-level attacks – tactics which would certainly result in unacceptable rates of attrition if employed against Warsaw Pact forces with their huge SAM resources. An all-weather variant was designed but it was never adopted. And it is extremely unlikely that the A-10 pilots would have sufficient experience, if forced to fly at low level in the sort of bad weather conditions often prevalent over West Germany. This problem has never been resolved and, despite the aircraft's popularity both with its pilots and the general public, funding was abruptly terminated in 1982 after the production of 707 models. No new tank-killers are planned for the immediate future.

Left: Arguably the best all-weather, long-range attack aircraft,the General Dynamics F-111 has been converted by Grumman into the EF-111A Raven and equips the only dedicated EW force in Western Europe, a USAF squadron at RAF Upper Heyford, England.

Below: The Harrier's great versatility enables it to operate away from prepared airstrips. Here, guarded by a member of the RAF Regiment, ground crew prepare a British Aerospace Harrier GR 3 for a mission, under the camouflage nets of a hide.

The F-111

With the final demise of the British Vulcan medium bomber, last used with mixed success in the Falklands war, the General Dynamics F-111 became the largest NATO deep-penetration aircraft and still remains the only true all-weather strike aircraft in the USAF arsenal. Few aircraft could have suffered so many teething problems, financial, technical and structural, as the F-111. Equipped with the first swing-wing in the world, side-by-side seating for the pilot and navigator (who can also be a qualified pilot), a small internal weapons bay and huge fuel facilities, this exceptional aircraft is capable of speeds of Mach 2.2 – yet can operate from soft airstrips even when carrying a full payload of 31,500 lbs (14,175 kg). At present two squadrons of F-111Es and Fs are based with the USAF in Great Britain: the 20th TFW at Upper Heyford, and the 48th TFW at Lakenheath. All F-111Ds operate from the continental United States.

Despite the notorious unreliability of the F-111 (it requires more man-hours per mile flown to maintain and repair than any other NATO aircraft), the basic airframes are deemed suitable for intensive combat until the year 2010. A highly expensive avionics modernization program is presently underway to upgrade the system's performance whilst reducing maintenance. In all it is hoped to upgrade 381 aircraft between December 1986 and 1992 after which they will boast the most modern of electronics, enabling them to be able to sustain extremely high damage tolerance whilst looking similar to the original.

Once the mainstay of several European air forces, the Lockheed F-104 Starfighter is now being relegated from its original fighter-bomber role by the F-16 and Tornado. But the F-104S advanced interceptor is likely to remain in service with the Italian and Turkish air forces for some time. Unfortunately this aircraft will always be known within Europe as "the flying coffin", due to the number of fatalities sustained by the Luftwaffe when operating it.

The Sepecat Jaguar is still in French and British service, but its days must be considered numbered. The British Jaguar S is fitted with digital inertial/attack systems, a laser ranger and marked target systems, but its limited poor-weather operational ability will always be a hindrance to its achieving a truly close-support role.

Harrier

The British Harrier is still, after 20 years in service, the only operational VTOL (vertical take-off and lift) in NATO, and is far superior to "Forger", its Warsaw Pact equivalent. Recent updates have been extensive enough to produce virtually a new aircraft, with 328 entering service with the US Marines, and a further 60 (designated Harrier GR5) with the Royal Air Force in Germany. Both are fitted with the latest Hughes angle rate bombing system which utilizes a combination of television and laser wavelengths to acquire, track and destroy surface targets; it has advanced navigation, altitude/heading reference systems and chaff/flare dispensers. The British GR5 is also fitted with an excellent, if expensive, Marconi-integrated defense system. Both systems carry externally-mounted 25-mm guns and up to 9,200 lbs (4,140 kg) of stores or munitions on seven hard-points. This extremely versatile aircraft would deploy to "hard-standings" in time of impending hostilities thus making itself a difficult preemptive target.

Tornado

Arguably the most exciting aircraft to enter NATO service recently has been the Panavia Tornado multirole combat/strike aircraft. Powered by two Turbo-Union RB 199 turbofans, armed with two 27-mm Mauser cannon and equipped with seven

Left: Capable of operating from roads or rough strips, the SPECAT Jaguar was a joint venture between France and the UK. Jaguar is a useful and versatile all-weather attack aircraft in close-support or antiship roles.

Below: Shown here are three F-104G Lockheed Starfighters of the Netherlands air force. Once the mainstay of a number of NATO air forces, both as a strike aircraft and interceptor, the Starfighter will be used for years to come.

Top: Principally used as an advanced trainer, the Dassault-Breguet/Dornier Alpha Jet also has a light strike/reconnaissance role carrying a cannon and 5,500 lbs (2,500 kg) of weapons but it lacks the sophisticated avionics and ECM fit of more specialist aircraft.

Right: Replacing the MiG-21 as the Warsaw Pact's principle fighter, MiG-23 Flogger, seen here armed with AA-7 Apex and AA-8 Aphid medium- and short-range AAMs, has variable-geometry wings to improve payload and endurance.

COMPARISON OF YAK-36 FORGER AND BRITISH AEROSPACE HARRIER

	Forger	Harrier
Engine	One vector-thrust turbojet rated at 17,500 lbs (7,000 kg) thrust and two lift jets situated in the forward fuselage each rated at 8,000 lbs (3,100 kg)	One Rolls Royce Pegasus 103 vectored-thrust turbojet rated at 21,500 lbs (9,675 kg) thrust.
Weights		
(Empty)	18,000 lbs (8,100 kg)	13,600 lbs (6,120 kg)
(Maximum)	25,500 lbs (11,500 kg)	26,000 lbs (11,700 kg)
Dimensions		
(Span)	24 ft (7.2 m)	25 ft 3 ins (7.6 m)
(Length)	50 ft (15 m)	57 ft 3 ins (17.2 m)
(Height)	14 ft 4 ins (4.3 m)	13 ft 8 ins (4.1 m)
(Wing Area)	170 sq ft (15.8 m^2)	201 sq ft (18.7 m^2)
Performance		
(Max. speed)	627 mph (1,003 k/h)	737 mph (1,179 k/h)
(Initial climb)	14,750 ft per min (4,430 m/min)	50,000 ft per min (VTOL) (15,000 m/min)
(Service Ceiling)	39,370 ft (11,810 m)	50,000 ft+ (15,000 m+)
(Combat Radius)		
lo-lo-lo	150 miles (240 km)	175 miles (280 km)
hi-lo-hi	23 miles (36.8 km)	260 miles (416 km)
Armament	Combination of GSh-23 gun pods, AA-8 Aphid close-range AAMS, rocket launchers or bombs totalling 3,000 lbs (1,350 kg) or AS-7 Kerry missiles	Combination of 30-mm cannon, Sidewinder missiles, up to 2,000 lbs (900 kg) of stores or bombs

external pods, this futuristic aircraft can carry up to 18,000 lbs (8,100 kg) and is capable of speeds of Mach 1.2 at sea level and Mach 2.2 at height. Equipped with forward-looking and terrain-following radar, head-up and head-down displays, the aircraft is fully stable at low level. No other aircraft within NATO can deliver so large a load in a long-range, all-weather, blind, first-pass mission as the Tornado IDS (interdiction strike) aircraft. Entry into Royal Air Force service has been somewhat delayed by sales to Oman and Saudi Arabia. Nevertheless, over 420 Tornadoes had been delivered by the end of 1985 and over 200 more were on order.

With the introduction of Tornado, the rebuilt F-111 and later variants of the F-16, NATO is amassing a considerable force of strike aircraft. On the basis that they are not destroyed on the ground within minutes of an outbreak of war, these aircraft could play a considerable part in the planned engagement and destruction of the Warsaw Pact's armored masses.

Fighter Aircraft

Warsaw Pact

Although several new aircraft have recently entered Soviet service, the MiG-21 Fishbed remains the principal aircraft of the Warsaw Pact, despite its low-speed, lack of performance and complex construction. Designed originally as a lightly-armed air-superiority fighter, the first production model carried a simple sound-ranging sight, two 30-mm cannon and two Atoll air-to-air missiles. The R-11 engine left the aircraft dangerously underpowered and it was not until 1959 and the arrival of the MiG-21F variant with its new, uprated Turmansky R-11F-300 engine and reduced armament, that production began in earnest.

The MiG-21 is essentially a clear-weather low-payload fighter, but it has been exported worldwide and is even produced under license in China where it is designated the F7. Over 750 models are in service with Soviet frontal aviation, 350 with Poland, 300 with Czechoslovakia, 200 with East Germany and 150 with Romania. The introduction of the MiG-21PF in 1961 added a limited all-weather potential, but the redesigning of the cockpit that had to be carried out considerably reduced the pilot's vision. The latest variant, the MiG-21 SMT, which first flew in 1973, incorporates an improved gunsight and enhanced avionics. It is capable of carrying the AA-8 Aphid air-to-air missile, but would prove no match for the advanced NATO fighters it would be likely to encounter and, in the event of a conflict, would probably be relegated to deep area defense.

Flogger B

Far more advanced, if less prevalent outside the Soviet Union, is the MiG-23 Flogger B. There are currently 2,000 models in the USSR and, at its peak, production was running at a rate of 300 per annum. Originally, Flogger B was envisaged as a counter to the new generation of NATO aircraft, epitomized by the F-4 Phantom, and models featured a larger wing area with far greater resultant stability and maneuverability. This aircraft now forms the backbone of Warsaw Pact interdiction. All Flogger Bs

are fitted with powerful "high lark" radar, and armed with missiles designed for medium-range combat and dogfighting. A laser sighting/ranging aid is carried beneath the nose.

A later air-defense derivative, designated Flogger G, is powered by a new Turmansky R-29B engine, affording a maximum speed in excess of Mach 2.2. Flogger G has the ability to jettison overload fuel tanks when required and is fitted with a much improved pulse-doppler radar capable of directing missiles against lower-altitude targets. Unusually for an air-defense aircraft, Flogger G will apparently engage an enemy at radar range, closing in for short-range-missile or cannon engagement only as a last resort. The Soviets must therefore either have complete faith in their IFF abilities or believe that their numerical superiority is so great that losses due to misidentification are acceptable.

New interceptors

Three completely new interceptors have entered Soviet service in the last five years. There is little hard information available on the MiG-29 Fulcrum. It has an estimated top speed of Mach 2.3 and probable range of 500 miles (800 km). The variable-geometry swing-wing of the early 1980s has been replaced by the conventional swing-wing. A combination of AA-2-2 Advanced Atoll missiles, AS-7, AS-10 and other missiles may be carried and Fulcrum is the first Soviet aircraft to have a full look-down shoot-down capability. The engine thrust/weight ratio is considered to be as good as any in NATO, and clearly Fulcrum will be taken very seriously by the Western powers. Another important feature is that Soviet pilots in action will be given very great latitude in taking decisions. Overall, Fulcrum has the potential to be a formidable adversary for years to come.

The MiG-31 Foxhound is a direct extension of the fast but unmaneuverable MiG-25 Foxbat reconnaissance aircraft. With speeds of up to Mach 2.3 and a combat range of 930 miles (1,500 km) as well as full look-down shoot-down radar capability, Foxhound is capable of intercepting the fastest NATO strike aircraft. Little is known about the armament of this enormous fighter, but it is believed that up to eight AA-6 Acrid or AA-9 missiles can be carried. Foxhound, a stretched version of the original Foxbat, is slower than Foxbat despite its larger engines, but far more maneuverable. Unusually for a fighter, Foxhound is a two-seater, with the pilot and navigator seated in tandem.

Larger than, but otherwise similar to the MiG-29, the Su-27 Flanker will certainly prove to be one of the world's outstanding combat aircraft well into the 21st century. Flanker, too, will have look-down shoot-down radar ability and will carry eight new AA-10 missiles. Little more is known about the aircraft or the missiles it will carry. Very probably, the AA-10 will have a range comparable to that of US Phoenix, that is, 124 miles (200 km). It is reckoned that Flanker has a top speed of Mach 2.35 and high-altitude range of 715 miles (1,150 km).

Soviet frontal aviation tactics have changed recently to allow pilots more scope and discretion. To operate with total efficiency, however, interceptors like the Su-27 and MiG-29 would require the support of early warning and control aircraft to overcome jamming, to differentiate between genuine and deception targets and to steer the fighter towards its target. The Soviet fleet of Tu-126 Moss aircraft would not be up to the task, while the very capable Ilyushin Mainstay-A, based on the IL-76 freighter, is so expensive that only four a year are being built. Thus, for some time to come, the best Soviet aircraft will be frustrated by their own air force's sheer inability to offer sufficient targets.

NATO

In time of war NATO interceptors would aim to pick off enemy strike aircraft at maximum range, if possible, without engaging the covering fighters. Recent advances in Soviet air-to-air

Left: For many years the backbone of Warsaw Pact air defense, the Mikoyan-Gurevich MiG-21 Fishbed is still effective and remains in service with Warsaw Pact airforces even after the introduction of more modern fighters.

Below: A potential threat to any NATO aircraft, the MiG-29 Fulcrum, with its all-weather capability, is illustrated here armed with the modern AA-10 AAM, flying above a Soviet Backfire bomber.

The Dassault-Breguet Mirage 2000 follows in a long line of French deltas as a multirole fighter though its chief role is that of air-superiority. It is seen here armed with two 30-mm cannon, two Matra Super 530 and two Matra 550 Magic AAMs.

missiles, however, have so reduced NATO's advantage in this field that it is now conceded that fighter-to-fighter clashes would be inevitable. Europe is currently producing excellent interceptors, but by far the largest number are operated by the USAF who hope, by 1990, to have 40 tactical fighter systems, including the AIM-120 Advanced Medium Air-to-Air Missile (AMRAAM) and the fancifully-named "Low-Altitude Navigation and Targeting Infrared System for Night" (LANTIRN). These will be fitted to the F-15 and F-16 fleets to provide a multishot beyond visual range capability, coupled with a much improved search potential.

Phantom

Within NATO numerous new aircraft have been introduced in the last decade and many existing models have been completely updated. Despite its age, the McDonnell Douglas F4 Phantom is still formidable, and out of the 5,195 originally built, some 2,700 are presently in service. Phantom, of which numerous variants exist, combines durability, good range and payload. Most also now carry the Westinghouse AWG-10 or APQ-120 radars. With a maximum speed of Mach 2.27 at high level or Mach 1.19 at low level, when fitted with Sparrow missiles, all models are capable of carrying four AIM-7 Sparrow or AMRAAM air-to-air missiles recessed under the fuselage, and a further two AIM-7 Sparrows or four AIM-9 Sidewinder missiles on external pods. The external pods can support a weight of 16,000 lbs (7,250 kg) comprising fuel tanks and bombs or other munitions.

Although most European nations operate the F-4E fighter, West Germany chose the simpler F-4F model without provision either for Sparrow missiles or for certain sophisticated EW equipment. Britain operates two variants, the F-4K (Phantom FG-1) for the Royal Navy and F-4M (Phantom FGR-2) for the

Top right: The Sukhoi Su-15 Flagon, seen here armed with AA-3 Anah AAM, serves as an all-weather interceptor to defend the borders of the Soviet Union. It gained notoriety as the aircraft that shot down Korean Air Lines Flight 007 in 1983.

Center: Designed to combat the US Valkyrie bomber, which was later cancelled, the MiG-25 Foxbat has a top speed in excess of Mach 3, shown here armed with AA-6 Acrid AAMs.

Right: In the 1970s, Belgium, Denmark, the Netherlands and Norway ran a competition for a new multirole fighter. This was won by the General Dynamics F-16 Fighting Falcon, shown here in Belgian livery.

RAF, both with Spey engines which have proved disappointing at top speed and high altitudes. At present, McDonnell Douglas, in conjunction with Pratt & Whitney, are offering a major refit package that will keep Phantom in service in the next century. A new PW 1120 engine, similar to that fitted to the F-16, affords additional thrust with lower fuel consumption, while a new 916-gallon (242 liter) fuel tank enhances range. A Hughes multimode radar, trialled successfully in the F-18 Hornet, and a GEC Avionics air-data computer, as fitted to the F-16C, are also incorporated.

Tornado

The Tornado ADV (Air-Defense Variant) was originally designed by the British to replace its Phantoms as a protector of domestic airspace. It has, however, proved so successful that it is now attracting a great deal of export interest. The ADV (designated Tornado F2) is arguably the most successful long-range interceptor in NATO, outperforming all Warsaw Pact aircraft except the MiG-25 and MiG-31 in straight-line speed. It is 80 per cent similar in design to the established IDS version, is extremely economical in fuel, and is equipped with the latest electronics such as the Foxhunter look-up look-down radar and missile-guidance system. Armed with four Skyflash missiles and two Sidewinder missiles carried in the fuselage, the F-2 will be capable of carrying the latest technology AIM-120A AMRAAM and ASRAAM missiles and will very probably play a leading role in European defense for decades to come.

Top right: A Northrop F-5 of the Netherlands. Although this American designed aircraft has never been adopted by the USA except in small numbers for aggressor squadrons, it has operated successfully in most of NATO's air forces as a cheap and simple fighter and remains in service to this day.

Right: Armed with four AIM-7 Sparrow and four AIM-9 Sidewinder AAMs two of the USAF's principal air-superiority fighter, the McDonnell Douglas F-15 Eagle, fly a combat air patrol over the Alaskan mountains. The photograph was taken from a third Eagle.

Above: AMX is a joint Italian and Brazilian aircraft tasked with close air support, battlefield interdiction and reconnaissance. It will be used by the Italians to replace their F-104G Starfighters and Aeritalia (Fiat) G-91s.

Above: A McDonnell Douglas F-18 Hornet captured firing a salvo of rockets. At first intended as carrier-based, Hornet is now used as a land-based dual-role fighter and strike aircraft and has been bought by Spain and Canada.

Right: Britain's Panavia Tornado ADV was developed from the IDS variant to fulfill the RAF's requirement for a long-range, all-weather interceptor capable of remaining for a long time on station, far from base.

The F-15 and F-18

The McDonnell Douglas F-15 Eagle is currently replacing the F-106, and will soon replace the F-4 in its role of protecting the United States. At present, 15 squadrons of F-15s, of which 10 are manned by the Air National Guard, are tasked with this role. Sixty F-15s, built in 1986, together with 42 more aircraft planned, are capable of operating the AIM-120 AMRAAM. All F-15C and D variants are being retrofitted with an improved Hughes radar, while doppler beam-sharpening techniques give a much higher air-to-ground mapping resolution, with large-range discrimination of targets while flying in a tight formation.

Designed originally as a naval replacement for the A-7, the F-18 Hornet has proved itself a highly versatile land-based fighter with excellent dogfighting potential. It is relatively small, thoroughly reliable and easy to maintain. Hornet is armed with a 20-mm M61 gun and equipped with nine external pylons with a maximum load of 13,400 lbs (6,100 kg) for a mixture of bombs and Sparrow missiles. In addition, a Sidewinder can be fixed on the tip of each wing. Hornet's acceleration gives it an advantage in a high-level dogfight, but its lack of terrain-following radar and large, wide-span fixed-wing make it vulnerable at low altitudes, and its rather limited radius with full weapons load is a further disadvantage. In 1984, structural weaknesses were discovered, which comparatively simple modifications have since rectified. The export potential of this fine aircraft is just beginning to be exploited.

NATO superiority

NATO is superior to the Warsaw Pact in virtually every aspect of fighter aircraft. In the late 1960s, the North Vietnamese "kill" rate was marginally superior to that of the USAF, but this was because of localized hit-and-run tactics, which would certainly

Above: Designed as a single-seat air superiority fighter, the F-15 Eagle has evolved into a twin seater dual-role fighter capable of carrying 24,500 lbs (11,100 kg) of bombs and, as seen here, four Sidewinder SAMs.

Douglas F-4 Phantom shown flying over West Germany, armed with four Sparrow and four Sidewinder AAMs. Phantom is the classic multirole aircraft of the last 25 years, operating from land or carriers.

If required, Aeroflot could support military transport aviation with the many and varied aircraft at its disposal. Shown from second left to right, the Antonov An-400 Condor, Tupolev Tu-154 Careless and Yakovlev Yak-42 Clobber.

Above: On board a NATO-operated Boeing E-3A AWACS aircraft. An American operator communicates with a ground command center through a digital display, while next to him a West German monitors a control panel.

not prevail in crowded European skies. However, the Warsaw Pact has always boasted excellent missiles of all kinds, and has now developed radar to exploit these to the full. It will only be when a new generation of US missiles is introduced that NATO superiority will be reestablished. Even so, the Soviets' shooting down of the Korean airliner in 1983 suggests that their communications are still inadequate and their chain of command confused. In this case, NATO would have the considerable advantage in any future conflict of speed, surprise and versatility.

Military Transport Aircraft

Warsaw Pact

The Military Transport Aviation of the Soviet Union (VTA) operates some 1,200 aircraft, from the small An-Colt – capable of carrying 12 passengers or up to 3,306 lbs (1,488 kg) of freight – to the huge An-124 Condor now entering service.

Above: The Antonov An-12 Cub is the Warsaw Pact's equivalent of the West's Hercules, a general purpose freighter that can operate from rough, short airstrips. Cub can also be fitted with twin 23-mm cannons in the rear turret.

Virtually all aircraft emanate from the Antonov design bureau and are also in civilian service with Aeroflot. Design costs are therefore reduced considerably, whilst the Air Force has a constant reserve of domestic aircraft and pilots. Operationally the VTA is directly subordinate to the Soviet General Staff, thus making its facilities readily accessible. It has several diverse responsibilities including the transportation of airborne units, the movement of major weapon systems, nuclear missiles, ammunition and casualty evacuation; it would indeed be hard-pressed to fulfill all its functions in time of war. Although the Soviet Army boasts eight airborne divisions, the VTA would experience difficulty in simultaneously transporting more than two full divisions with basic equipment.

The VTA practices its vast lift potential in all major exercises. It played a crucial role in the Yom Kippur War of 1973, when 15,000 tons of material were airlifted to the Egyptian and Syrian armies. But it has never been tested in a hostile environment. During the invasion of Czechoslovakia in 1968, for instance, five squadrons of An-12 Cubs needed one whole night to land the 103rd Guards Air Assault Division at Prague Airport. Most airborne troops used in the invasion of Afghanistan were moved by land rather than run the risk of transport by air, securing the airports and flight paths.

All Soviet transport aircraft are built to a rugged design to reduce maintenance requirements, with several carrying their own maintenance crews for long-term out-of-area operations. All have large, rugged undercarriages and integrated winches capable of moving cargo without recourse to an external power source. And all but the largest have excellent short take-off and lift (STOL) capabilities, enabling them to operate independently from the numerous, roughly-made airstrips that abound in the Eastern bloc. Rather strangely, many of the transports (notably the An-12 Cub) do not have pressurized cargo cabins – thus considerably lowering their operation ceilings when carrying troops.

Bottom right: The Antonov An-22 Cock, with its long-range and large payload, has demonstrated its effectiveness by delivering vast quantities of arms and ammunition to Soviet allies in different parts of the world.

Similar in appearance to Lockheed's C-141, the Ilyushin Il-76 Candid would be capable of flying in reinforcements and stores close to the front, in support of operations conducted anywhere in the Warsaw Pact.

Possibly the most versatile aircraft since the DC-3, Lockheed's C-130 Hercules acts as the transport workhorse for many airforces and in a number of specialist roles from gunship in Vietnam, through SAR to inflight refueller.

The An-12 Cub

The An-12 four-engined turboprop is an important element in the VTA but is now being replaced by the far superior IL-76 Candid at the rate of approximately 30 aircraft a year. Capable of airlifting 90 troops, 60 paratroopers or up to 44,200 lbs (19,890 kg) of cargo, the An-12 has a range (with maximum payload) of 1,832 miles (2,931 km). In line with Soviet policy, it is fitted with a twin 23-mm tail-gun, though the effectiveness of this must be considered doubtful. And though it is still used extensively by airborne troops – between 90 and 115 aircraft are required to lift a complete BMD-equipped airborne regiment – the An-12 is incapable of carrying larger support items, such as engineering plant. Approximately 250 of these aircraft are still in operation with the VTA and a further 20 with the Polish Air Force.

The smaller twin turboprop An-24 Coke, with its maximum payload of 10,168 lbs (4,576 kg) and range of 1,860 miles (2,976 km), remains in service throughout the Warsaw Pact. Approximately 100 are within the Soviet Union, but are likely to be replaced by the AN-72 Coaler with its much improved range, speed and capacity.

The An-22 Cock, of which some 50 are in Soviet service, can carry 175 troops or 176,800 lbs (79,560 kg) of cargo to a range of 2,550 miles (4,080 km). Used mainly for air landings rather than air-dropping, the An-22 Cock is, despite its huge taíl-gate capable of transporting four BMDs or a variety of all but the largest equipment. It would almost certainly be used in large-scale airborne operations to provide deliveries of equipment and reinforcement personnel.

Bottom left: Divided by the expanse of the Atlantic, NATO allies would have to rely on aircraft such as this Lockheed C-141 Starlifter to transport urgently required reinforcements and equipment.

Below: McDonnell's KC-10A Extender, seen here refuelling an F-16 Fighting Falcon, can carry passengers and cargo over 4,000 miles (6,400 km) when fully loaded. Such a capability is necessary to reinforce operations worldwide where no bases are available en route.

Above: French Mirage F1-Cs queuing up behind a Boeing KC-135F dual-purpose transport/tanker for refuelling. In-flight refuelling is an important element in extending the capabilities of any aircraft type, whether transport, strike or fighters.

Right: The Lockheed C-5B Galaxy, seen here on its maiden flight in 1985. With its long range, large payload and, most importantly, unobstructed height, width and length of the lower deck, Galaxy offers the USAF an invaluable capability to support overseas operations.

A COMPARISON OF WARSAW PACT AND NATO TRANSPORT AIRCRAFT

Aircraft	Maximum Range (miles/km) with Full Payload	Maximum Payload (lbs/kg)	Landing Run (ft/m)	Take Off Run (ft/m)
C-5 Galaxy	3,100/4,960	245,000/110,250	2,950/885	8,000/2,400
C-130H Hercules	2,100/3,360	43,500/19,575	1,750/525	4,700/1,410
C-141 Starlifter	2,780/4,450	74,200/33,400	1,900/570	5,000/1,500
C-160 Transall	2,750/4,400	35,300/15,890	2,300/690	2,950/885
AN-12	1,830/2,930	44,100/19,850	2,820/846	2,790/840
AN-22 Cock	5,900/9,440	176,350/79,360	?	3,300/990
IL-76 Candid	3,500/5,600	88,000/39,600	1,500/450	2,800/840

In conjunction with DOSAFF, VTA is responsible for pilot training from basic glider-flying to operational conversion standard and is equipped with a wide variety of aircraft including twin-seater operational fighters.

NATO

Geography always poses problems, particularly in time of war – when NATO would have to move huge reinforcements of men and equipment across the North Atlantic as quickly as possible. A large percentage of NATO troops are concentrated in huge barracks in their home countries, and will have to be brought forward to their war positions within hours of a war breaking out if these positions are not to be overrun immediately.

Before the Vietnam War, the United States relied heavily on its seapower for transportation, and still tends to utilize the US Navy for freight movement whenever possible. Since the late 1960s, however, emphasis has been given to the improvement of long-range airlift, so much so that during a single month in 1973 the USAF was able to lift 22,000 tons of weaponry and ammunition from the United States to Israel in less than 600 sorties.

The majority of the USAF transport fleet is based permanently within the United States, with less than 50 C-130 Hercules based in Europe and the Pacific. Maintained in a state of constant readiness, it is capable of transporting units as large as the 82nd Airborne Division anywhere in the world on minimal notice.

The current US airlift potential combines elements of the regular USAF, Air National Guard (ANG), Air Force Rescue (AFRes) and the Civil Reserve Air Fleet (CRAF). Combined airlift capacity is presently in the region of 32.4 million tons/miles per day. Despite being vastly superior to the combined Warsaw Pact potential, this is now considered inadequate and is being increased, under the auspices of the Airlift Improvement Program (AIP), to 66 million tons/miles per day. Many modern loads are bulky rather than heavy, so that many highly-powered aircraft, although full on take-off, nevertheless have vast payload reserves. This wastefulness is being overcome by "stretching" the cargo areas to enable them to hold greater bulk without interference to the payload.

At present the Regular Air Force would expect to transport more than 50 per cent of all inter-theater tonnage, and more than 60 per cent into the actual war zones. The majority of the residue would be carried by civil airlines under the Civil Reserve Air Fleet scheme, but this is proving unpopular with the commercial airlines. Out of 450-plus wide-bodied transport aircraft in the US civilian fleet, less than 100 are all-cargo versions, or are even capable of freight-cargo modifications. The Government has expressed its willingness to compensate the airlines for the additional costs involved in the purchase and maintenance of aircraft capable of modification, but this has had little effect to date.

Galaxy

The largest and most advanced heavy weightlifter presently in service is the Lockheed C-5A Galaxy. The USAF has 70 of these most versatile aircraft, which is capable of carrying 270

troops or 245,000 lbs (110,250 kg) of cargo a range of 3,875 miles (6,200 km). Recent wing improvements have quadrupled its life expectancy to 30,000 flying hours, making the Galaxy likely to remain in service into the 21st century.

Hercules

Without doubt the most famous transport aircraft still in production is the C-130 Hercules, known affectionately to those who have flown in it as the "Hurky Bird". First produced as long ago as 1954, the latest models (designated C-130 H-30) have a stretched fuselage increasing the length by 14.7 ft (4.4 m) and the cargo areas by 40 per cent. During the last two decades the C-130 Hercules has become the standard medium-range transport in most NATO air forces. Belgium, for instance, operates 12 (stretched), Canada 28, Denmark 3 (stretched), Greece 12 (stretched), Great Britain 54 (plus six tankers), Italy 13, Norway 6 (stretched) and the United States in excess of 1,000. The UK, which has recently reestablished a parachute assault capability, experimented with the fitting of advanced navigational aids to the C-130 Hercules – and now boasts the ability to drop an entire battalion (with support) into a single Drop Zone (DZ) in less than 15 minutes.

The US C-141A Starlifter fleet has recently completed a major refit, during which all 285 aircraft were stretched by 24 ft 3 inches (7.38 m) and given an in-flight refuelling capacity. Even after extending the range of this veteran aircraft, the Starlifter is not technologically advanced enough to survive beyond the next decade.

The Boeing KC-135 has provided the USAF with its basic tanker fleet since the 1950s. Rather than replace these reliable old workhorses, the US government has improved their engines and fuel-dispensing capabilities, making them more likely to be retained in service into the 21st century. Over 20 KC-10A Extender tanker/cargo aircraft (variants of the DC-10 airliner) are now

operational, and are capable of transporting sufficient fuel to Europe to support over 200 fighters in less than three days.

Other NATO transport aircraft

The UK operates a fleet of six C-130 tankers, as well as 22 converted Victor K2s and a small but growing number of converted VC10s and Tristar 500s. Having considerable out-of-area commitments, the UK maintains a tanker fleet considerably larger than that required to fulfill its NATO responsibilities. In wartime, this surplus would prove invaluable in enhancing the speedy stockpiling of US fuel in Europe.

France and West Germany have reopened the C-160 Transall production line to meet a French requirement for 25 additional aircraft. It has been suggested that these aircraft are being built to provide employment within the state-controlled Aerospatiale Corporation rather than fulfill a military need. But there can be no doubt that these additional aircraft would still provide excellent additional medium-range lift capability in an emergency.

NATO transport aircraft, particularly in the field of in-flight refuelling, are far in advance of their Warsaw Pact rivals. But large and comparatively slow transports are highly vulnerable and will be able to operate only if adequate air cover is provided. It is the potential lack of this fighter cover, rather than a lack of transports as such, which may prove critical in the future.

A joint venture between France and Germany produced the C-160 Transall, a medium transport aircraft capable of carrying 35,000 lbs (16,000 kg) of cargo, or up to 93 troops, or a lesser number of paratroops or stretcher cases.

Strategic Nuclear Weapons

Land-based Strategic Missiles

Warsaw Pact

The Rakejnyye Voyska Strategicheskovo Naznacheniya (Strategic Rocket Forces) of the Soviet Union are the most powerful and secretive arm of the Red Army. Most available information is deduced either from the numerous parades held in the Soviet Union, from disclosures made during the preambles to various summits, and from information deliberately or accidentally leaked to Western intelligence sources. For this reason it is perfectly possible to read vastly differing reports from generally diverse and unauthoritative sources, all relating to the same equipment. What is known is that the Soviets tend to site their ICBM (Intercontinental ballistic missile) sites deep in the hinterland, following the line of the Trans-Siberian Railway as far as possible. A huge test center exists in the Plesetsk area, approximately halfway between Moscow and Leningrad.

Soviet land-based missiles have traditionally been deployed in four basic configurations: above-ground unprotected launch pads, above-ground protected sites, hardened underground silos and land mobile systems. Initially, strategic missiles such as the medium-range SS-4 and SS-5 were deployed in clusters of soft above-ground launch sites, each consisting of four separate missile launchers, each with a single reload. This was good for replenishment and maintenance but it left the sites highly vulnerable to the new generations of US ICBMs, with the result that over 130 SS-4s and SS-5s were subsequently redeployed in hardened shelters.

Many of the latest missiles are transportable; this does not

Far left: The growing accuracy of ICBMs has increased their ability to knock out enemy missiles before launch, making silo-based systems such as this Soviet one more vulnerable to a pre-emptive strike.

Left: Capable of being deployed on and off the road on massive wheeled transporter-erector-launcher vehicles, the SS-X-25 ICBM would have a good chance of surviving an attack to launch a second reload. In this illustration TELs are in garages with vast sliding roofs.

The SS-20 LRINF greatly increased Soviet capability with its superior accuracy, 3 MIRVs and substantially greater range, posing a threat that Pershing II and GLCMs can hardly balance.

mean, however, that they will be shifted here and there around the countryside looking for launch sites, but they will be moved away from the parent base in time of crisis to frustrate a preemptive attack.

The SS-17

Approximately 150 SS-17 ICBMs are presently deployed. Capable of carrying either four 0.75 MT (one megaton is equivalent to 1 million tons of TNT) warheads or a single highly accurate 3.6 MT warhead for targeting against US silos, the SS-17 is "cold-launched". This means that the missile is ejected from its silo by a powerful gas-generator and does not engage its own first-stage motors until it is above the ground. Minimum damage is therefore sustained by the silo which can be reused within a matter of days. In a 1980 exercise it is reported that over 40 silos were reloaded within two to five days, implying that these silos would have to be targeted by NATO even after firing, to ensure that they were not used for a second Soviet attack.

The SS-18

The SS-18 is the largest missile in service in the world. It has a maximum stated range of up to 10,000 miles (16,000 km) and is armed with two types of warhead: a single warhead of 18–25 MT and an MIRV (Multiple Independently-targeted Reentry Vehicle) variant, each with eight to ten independently-targeted missiles of 1 to 2 MT. With a throw-weight of 15,014 lbs (6,760 kg), the huge SS-18 is ten times the size of the US Minuteman III and twice the size of Titan II.

The SS-X-25

Deployment of the new SS-X-25 three-stage medium-weight ICBM is also continuing, with the first missile now operational. It is expected that eventually 460 of these missiles will be deployed, either in existing SS-13 silos hidden among SS-20 launchers or, rather more fancifully, deployed on railway trucks around the countryside. NATO originally thought that up to nine MIRV would be carried on the SS-X-25; it is now considered that the Soviets have decided on a single, much larger warhead. The United States regards production of the SS-X-25 as a flagrant breach of both SALT agreements – but the deployment of this new 59 ft (17.7 m)-long missile, with its estimated range of 6,560 miles (10,496 km) continues unabated.

When the Soviet Union has completed the deployment of the SS-20 sites (approximately two-thirds of which are targeted against NATO and one-third against China), it will have deployed approximately 1,400 intermediate-range missile warheads – 1,250 of them mounted on SS-20s, and approximately 200 carried by obsolete SS-4s. The last SS-5s are now being phased out.

Deployment of medium-range missiles within Warsaw Pact satellite nations is currently underway, with the old SS-12 Scaleboard and later SS-22 also being moved from the Soviet Union to East Germany and Czechoslovakia. Despite the presence of both the SS-21 (range 75 miles/120 km) and the SS-22 (range 550 miles/880 km) in East Germany and Czechoslovakia, it is thought that their potential targets are duplicated by the SS-20s with their three MIRV – and that their presence is more political than strategic. Over 60 SS-20s are required to launch an attack against all major identifiable NATO targets in range, plus a further 300 to destroy all civilian targets.

The latest development of the type, the Delta IV nuclear-powered ballistic submarine is armed with 16 of the latest SS-N-23 SLBMs. These are also likely to replace the less effective SS-N-18s in Delta III submarines.

The Soviet Union has now deployed sufficient SS-20s to do both.

NATO

For many years the ICBM leg of the USA's strategic triad has consisted of 53 Titan II missiles, 450 single warhead Minuteman II and 550 Minuteman III missiles: a total of 1,054 launchers. The Titan II, designed during the Eisenhower administration as a counter to the increase in Soviet ICBMs, was the last large missile to be built by the United States. Despite Titan's age, the combination of its extreme accuracy plus its range of 9,320 miles and yield of 7.4 MT insured that this missile would remain in service for a long time, although the last Titan is due to be withdrawn in 1987. The US originally intended to construct 108 launchers in hardened underground silos, but only 54 missiles were eventually deployed in six squadrons, each with nine missiles. Following an accident in 1980, the number of missiles deployed was reduced to the present 53.

Minuteman

The Minuteman was designed at the end of the 1950s as a

smaller and simpler second-generation ICBM. Originally envisaged as a mobile system capable of operating from existing rail lines in the midwest USA, it was eventually deployed in fixed, hardened silos. Minuteman II became operational in 1966 as a replacement for the original Mk I; 450 are still in service, having recently undergone large-scale replacement of their components whose shelf-life had expired. The later Minuteman III entered service in 1970. Since production was completed in 1977, the force of 550 missiles has been continually updated with improved silos, better guidance software, a new guidance package and new reentry vehicles each with their own propulsion, forming an independent fourth stage to the missile. Not only can a missile now be launched within a minute – and retargeted within 30 minutes – but manpower is also reduced to a minimum to the extent that it would take less than 200 launch officers to launch the entire fleet of 1,000 missiles. At present an unspecified number of missiles are allocated to the Emergency Rocket Communications System, while it is intended to convert up to 100 Minuteman silos to take the long-overdue Peacekeeper Missile.

The MX (Peacekeeper)

Known originally as the MX missile, the Peacekeeper had a highly checkered career even before being deployed. Prior to the Carter administration it was decided to deploy the MX on road (not rail!) cars to enable it to be moved anywhere in the country in time of crisis. The Carter regime favored the MPS (Multiple Protective Shelter) scheme, but the Reagan

Left: A tomahawk cruise missile is fired from its camouflaged transporter-erector-launcher in a test flight at the Dugway range in Western Utah.

Below: High over the Pacific, Peacekeeper reentry vehicles pass through the clouds after traveling over 4,700 miles (7520 km) from Vandenburg Air Force Base in California, during a test firing of this latest and most powerful of US ICBMs.

administration scrapped this in 1981, preferring to use existing Minuteman silos. Despite strong pressure from the Senate Armed Services Committee to concentrate all missiles in a tiny area no more than four miles (6.4 km) across, it is now planned to deploy 100 Peacekeeper missiles in existing silos between 1986 and 1990, in the region of the F E Warren Air Force Base in Wyoming. Better command and control facilities will be fitted and shock isolation devices added, but it is not intended to harden the silos themselves. When eventually deployed, this four-stage missile will have a range of 6,900 miles (11,040 km) and an armament of ten MIRVs, each of 300 KT yield.

Tomahawk

A smaller, more controversial missile in the NATO arsenal is the Tomahawk GLCM (Ground-Launched Cruise Missile). Equipped with DSMAC (Digital Scene-Matching Area-Correlation) guidance, and armed with the latest W83 nuclear or thermonuclear warhead, it is intended to deploy 464 missiles within USAF bases in the Netherlands, Italy and West Germany; cruise missiles have already been deployed in the UK. Each missile is pretargeted and, once set, requires the minimum of maintenance. A canister is loaded upon a 33-ton general duties transporter/erector/launcher (TEL) carrying four missile tubes in a single container, which can be elevated to the desired height. Each Combat Flight Group comprises four TELs (16 missiles) and two LCCs (launch control centers). Both LCCs are carried on huge 36-ton trucks; each is geared to leave its home base for one of several top secret launch sites in time of national emergency. It is clear from the reaction of the Warsaw Pact bloc, supported by domestic left-wing organizations around Europe, that the cruise missile, as it is widely known, is regarded by them as an excellent deterrent.

Pershing II

The Pershing I missile was originally deployed in 1962, and subsequently updated to the Ia standard presently in service with the West German Luftwaffe. The entire system is carried on four vehicles and is transportable by C-130 Hercules. With the aid of the Azimuth Reference System (ARS), the missile can be fired quickly from unsurveyed launch sites. The US 7th Army, originally equipped with the Pershing Ia, has now been re-equipped with the much improved Pershing II. Originally designed in 1974, entry into service was delayed by rocket propulsion problems for a further ten years but, nevertheless, it now provides NATO with its most accurate means of nuclear delivery.

In the Pershing II, the radar area-correlation guidance fitted inside the nose of the missile scans the ground as the warhead plunges towards its target – correlating the returns with stated target imagery and adjusting the course accordingly. The resultant pin-point accuracy reduces the tonnage of warhead required to 15 KT, thus extending the maximum range to 460

Vast Titan being launched from its hardened underground silo. Titan II is the largest of the US ICBMs and is scheduled to be replaced by Minuteman and MX by 1987.

miles (736 km). An "earth penetrator" device enables the warhead to "burrow" deep underground before exploding, making it more deadly in an attack against enemy missile silos and underground headquarters.

The S-3

France is the only other NATO power equipped with land-based nuclear missiles. Her 18 S-3 missiles are each capable of delivering a single 1.2 MT thermonuclear warhead at a range of 1,875 miles (3,000 km). It is the stated aim of the French government to replace its vulnerable fixed silos with either a strategic ballistic missile system, or its own cruise missile – but France is also dedicated to building a new independent class of nuclear submarine by the turn of the century, and may not be able to afford both.

Sea-Based Strategic Missiles

Warsaw Pact

The sea-based strategic missile force of the Soviet Navy has been greatly improved, both in effectiveness and survivability, under the influence of Admiral Gorshkov. The first true ballistic system consisted of the SS-N-4 Sark missile carried on a Zulu-class submarine, converted to carry two launchers in its conning tower. The short range of the SS-N-4 (435 miles/696 km), and the need of the submarine to surface to fire did not prevent the potential of the submarine-based system from being realized and the subsequent development encouraged.

The oldest nuclear missile submarine still in Soviet service is the Yankee I class, first introduced in 1967. In all, 34 Y-class boats were built between 1966 and 1974. Five have now been converted to cruise-missile carriers, while others are being phased out and replaced on a one-for-one basis by the latest Delta class. While this replacement policy is in accord with the SALT I agreement, it has, in fact, considerably enhanced Soviet firepower. Whereas the old Yankees were forced by lack of range to deploy relatively close to the US mainland, the new Deltas are able to cover most US strategic targets without leaving the protection of coastal waters.

Delta

The first submarines of the Delta class, built between 1973 and 1976 and designated Delta Is, were armed with the long-range SS-N-8 missile, capable of firing an 0.8 MT warhead over 5,600 miles (8,960 km). A stretched variant (designated Delta II), capable of transporting sixteen SS-N-8 launchers, appeared in 1976. But only four vessels of this class were built before the introduction of the Delta III, equipped with sixteen SS-N-18 launchers. The two-stage liquid fuel SS-N-18 (Mod 1), with its range of 4,040 miles (6,464 km), can carry three independently-targeted 200 kt warheads and, as such, is the first MIRV in Soviet submarine service. The Mod 2 missile has a single warhead and a range of 4,970 miles (7,952 km) and the latest Mod 3, a staggering seven MIRVs and range of 4,040 miles (6,464 km). Delta III submarines will be capable of operating from safe havens in the Barents Sea and Sea of Okhotsk. With a Circular Error Probability (CEP) as little as 1,539 yards (1,410 m), this formidable combination will inevitably play a key role in any future arms' treaties. (CEP is the radius of a circular area centered on a target, within which half of a given number of warheads fired at the target will fall.) A new SS-N-23 missile is currently entering service and is expected to replace the SS-N-18 in the next few years.

Typhoon

The Soviet Union has now launched a new class of vast submarines – the Typhoon class. Three times the size of the Delta III and 40 per cent larger than the US Ohio class, this

30,000-ton monster is armed with 20 of the latest SS-N-20 MIRVed SLBMs. With a range of 5,157 miles (8,251 km) each warhead contains six to nine MIRVs. There is little information to be had about this new missile – but it is known that four were fired simultaneously during a test in October, 1982.

Soviet ballistic missile submarines are currently deployed with three of the four fleets. Seventy per cent of them are based with the Northern Fleet at Murmansk; from where they patrol the Barents, Greenland and Norwegian Seas. Most of the remaining submarines are based with the Pacific Fleet at Petropavlovsk, near Vladivostok – while a small number of Golf IIs occasionally deploy with the Baltic Fleet.

Although the Soviet Union boasts a fleet in excess of 70 ballistic submarines, it is rare for more than 15 to be at sea at the

A French M-4 SLBM being launched from the experimental missile submarine Gymnote. When retrofitted to existing SSBNs and included in new ones, this missile will considerably enhance the French deterrent with its MIRVs and longer range.

same time. The Soviets would certainly not wish to have their fleet caught in port at the beginning of hostilities, and the unusual movement of a large number of ships to sea would be interpreted by NATO intelligence as a possible build-up for war.

NATO

With the exception of Britain's four submarines and France's *"force de frappe",* the US Navy operates NATO's entire seaborne deterrent. Until recently, the 31 boats of the Lafayette class were the cornerstone of US policy. Each armed with 16 Poseidon C-3 missiles and capable of a submerged speed of about 30 knots, twelve of this class have now been converted to take Trident C-4 missiles. And the huge Ohio-class submarines, purpose-built to carry 24 Trident missiles, are currently in production. With their unprecedented displacement of 18,700 tons, these were to be by far the largest submarines in world service – but they have now been completely overtaken by the Soviet Union's gigantic Typhoons of over 30,000 tons' displacement.

At present the US Navy is capable of keeping over 55 per cent of its nuclear fleet simultaneously at sea – which is far higher than Soviet numbers – and intends to increase this to 65 per cent in the future. The Trident missile has so great a range (4,225 miles/6,760 km, compared with 3,125 miles/5,000 km for Polaris) that it can be fired from safe home waters. And US communications and control systems are so far in advance of their Soviet equivalents that a sizable part of the fleet can operate from anywhere in the world, and still receive up-to-date information and instructions. Primary communications are provided by the TACAMO system; a C-130 Hercules, one of which is constantly airborne over the Atlantic and another over the Pacific, transmits on Very Low Frequency (VLF) using a 6.2 mile (9.9 km) trailing-wire antenna and a 100-kilowatt transmitter.

"Force de frappe"

The French deterrent, built at enormous cost, is entirely domestic and consists of five boats of the Le Redoutable class and a sixth, *L'Inflexible,* of more advanced design. Unlike Great Britain, which rarely has more than one submarine at sea at any one time, France aims at having three boats simultaneously at sea. Until recently, the French deterrent factor was considerably reduced by the fact that her missiles had only single reentry vehicles. But with the advent of the M-4 missile, with its five to seven MIRVs, each of 150 KT and range of 2,485 miles (4,000 km), the "*force de frappe*" is, indeed, a force to be reckoned with.

Polaris

The British fleet of four Resolution-class C-3 Polaris submarines is old by US standards, and a constant source of domestic political argument. The present British government plans to replace its fleet with four new Trident submarines, construction of which has recently begun – but it is possible that a future Labour government will scrap this project.

Poseidon

The Poseidon C-3 missile, although based on the Polaris (which is now operated only on the four British submarines), has at least equal the range, twice the payload and twice the accuracy. Since the conversion of twelve Lafayette-class submarines to Trident, 19 armed with Poseidon remain in service; there is no intention of scrapping these, or even updating them drastically, until the

Pershing II is a tactical missile system with a single nuclear warhead so accurate that it poses a threat to a number of hard targets within the western USSR.

late 1990s. At present the US fields some 496 Poseidon C-3/C-4 missiles out of a total of 640 missiles.

Trident

The Trident C-4 missile, with its enhanced range of 4,400 miles (7,040 km), first entered service with the USS *Francis Scott Key* in 1979 and is now operational with the Ohio class and 12 converted Lafayettes. A new longer-range and more accurate Trident II (D-5) is under development but, being longer in size than Trident I, will require a new submarine launch platform. At present the new British submarines under construction will take Trident II, but with a British front end – thus ensuring total domestic control.

The nuclear submarine fleets provide NATO with an excellent second-strike potential far superior to that of the Warsaw Pact. Furthermore, the existence of the British and French fleets, both totally independent, must convince the Soviet Union that waging an attack on Europe alone would inevitably lead to nuclear retaliations.

Strategic Defense Initiative

When President Reagan described his Strategic Defense Initiative – soon to be known as "Star Wars" – as a "vision of the future offering hope" in March 1983, he can have had little idea how much controversy his new-found policy of defensive warfare was about to cause. Whilst renowned scientists such as Edward Teller, the so-called "father of the H-bomb", have offered unequivocal support and influence to the scheme – such eminent militarists as Admiral Noel Gaylor, ex-C-in-C US Pacific Fleet, and politicians such as ex-Defense Secretary Schlesinger have attacked it. Proponents of the policy see it as the natural escape from "mutually assured destruction" (MAD); others see it as the plaything of over-excited academics, encouraged by unrelenting White House public relations.

The essence of Star Wars is simple. Without the defense initiative the following horrifying scenario is all too possible: 1,000 Soviet missiles are launched simultaneously in a first strike attack. Four minutes later, when the ICBMs are above the earth's atmosphere and heading for the United States, each rocket drops away leaving a container (called a "bus"), loaded with nuclear warheads and decoys. After approximately three more minutes the "bus" releases its warheads somewhere over the North Pole, each of which is directed by computer to its own target. Three minutes later, protected as far as possible by the decoys, the warheads start the "terminal phase" – reentering the earth's atmosphere and plummeting towards their targets. At present only Moscow, with its limited protective "shield" of Galosh anti-ballistic missiles, would have any chance to parry such an attack – and then only partially.

How Star Wars would work

It could be a different story with the introduction of a fully operational SDI system, comprising a layered system of defenses each with a possible combination of weapons. The 1,000 rockets would still take off – but would be immediately detected by satellites picking up the tremendous heat emitted on launch. Before the missiles would have time to leave the "boost phase" to enter the relative safety of outer space, and before

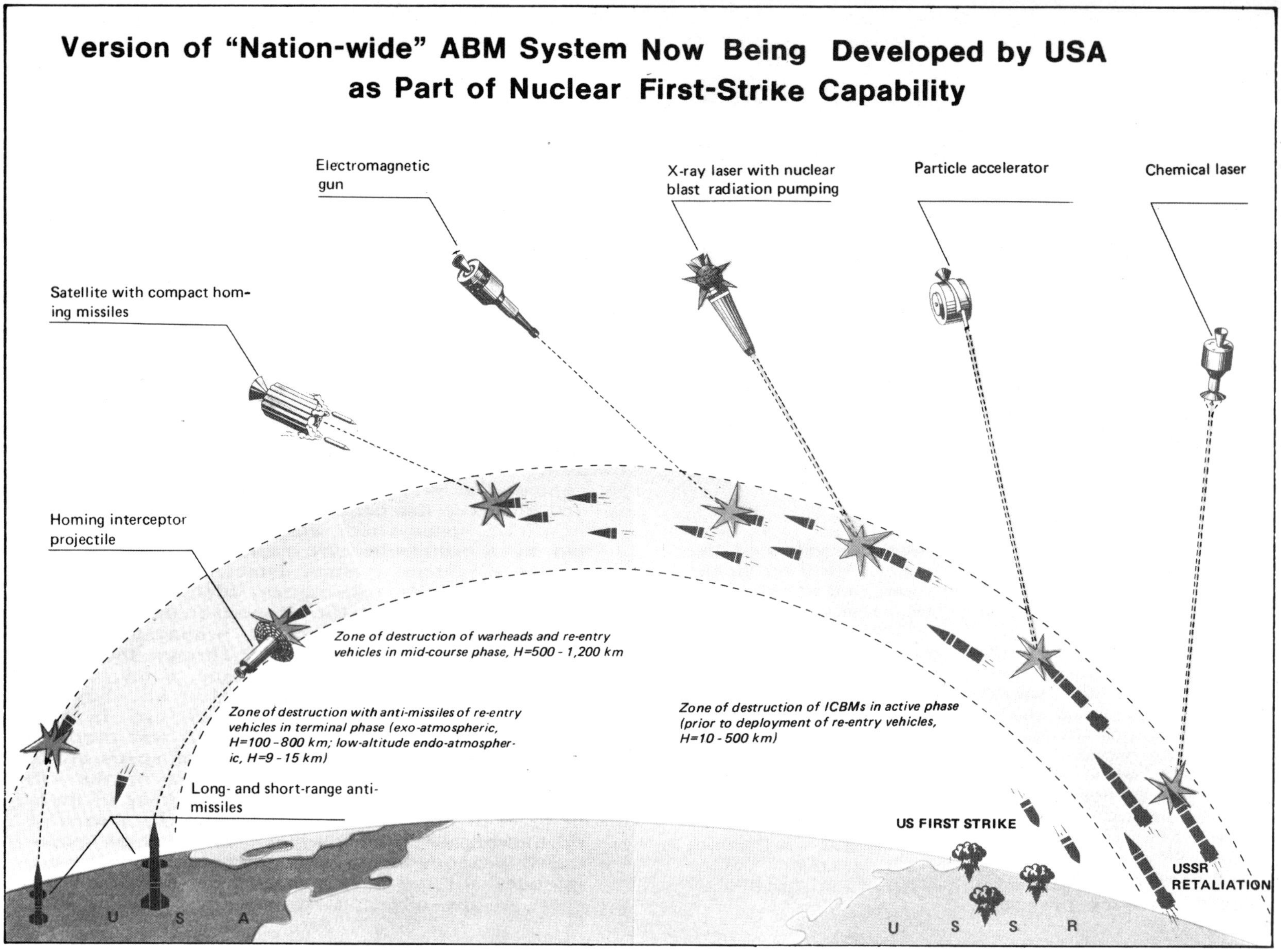

Version of "Nation-wide" ABM System Now Being Developed by USA as Part of Nuclear First-Strike Capability

they have deployed their warheads and decoys, an orbiting satellite armed with chemical laser guns could track and destroy them. Most of the missiles would be put out of action in the boost phase.

The missiles that get through this initial layer of defenses would then become the target for lasers carried on rockets fired from submarines. Any surviving this could then fall victim to earth-based lasers reflected off giant orbiting mirrors. These would be so precisely angled as not to diffuse the laser beam or, it is envisaged, be destroyed by kinetic energy projectiles fired from another satellite. Then a neutral particle beam, using concentrated atomic particles with no electrical charge, could be fired at the reentry vehicles of the incoming missiles to disrupt their internal electronics. As a last resort the final layer of defenses would come into effect with ground-based rockets or guns that could be launched or fired at any remaining missiles and dispersed warheads and decoys. The attack would have been thwarted.

The entire concept would sound utterly fanciful were it not for the fact that the US has budgeted $26 billion for research into the feasibility of SDI alone – even before making a definite commitment to put it into operation. Already millions of dollars have been spent; two of the early space shuttle missions were dedicated to it, six nuclear tests have taken place in the Nevada desert in 1985 simply to evaluate some of the ideas, and extensive research on the more exotic SDI technologies such as laser and particle beam weapons is underway at the Los Alamos and Lawrence Livermore weapons laboratories.

Pros and cons

It will be many years before it is known whether or not SDI is truly practicable and if so, whether it is truly welcome. It has raised many questions as to the effect it will have on the arms race and the militarization of space, whether it would give the US an offensive capability, plus the impact it will have on the current strategic balance between the two superpowers. While the Soviets have naturally reacted strongly against SDI, they have in fact been carrying out their own research for many years, and are nevertheless likely to feel threatened if the US should put a shield into place that could neutralize their own weapons before they are themselves able to set up similar protection, thus giving the US first-strike capability.

Above: Soviet representation of how SDI would work from the publication *Star Wars – Delusions and Dangers*. The diagram illustrates the principle of SDI with the various layers of defense.

Right: In September 1985 an F-15 Eagle successfully launched an ASAT antisatellite missile that intercepted its target, "killing" the satellite with the kinetic energy of a miniature homing vehicle.

An SDI defense system could include a space-based electromagnetic railgun (shown here in an artist's impression) that would fire hypervelocity projectiles to destroy nuclear-armed reentry vehicles.

USA
63

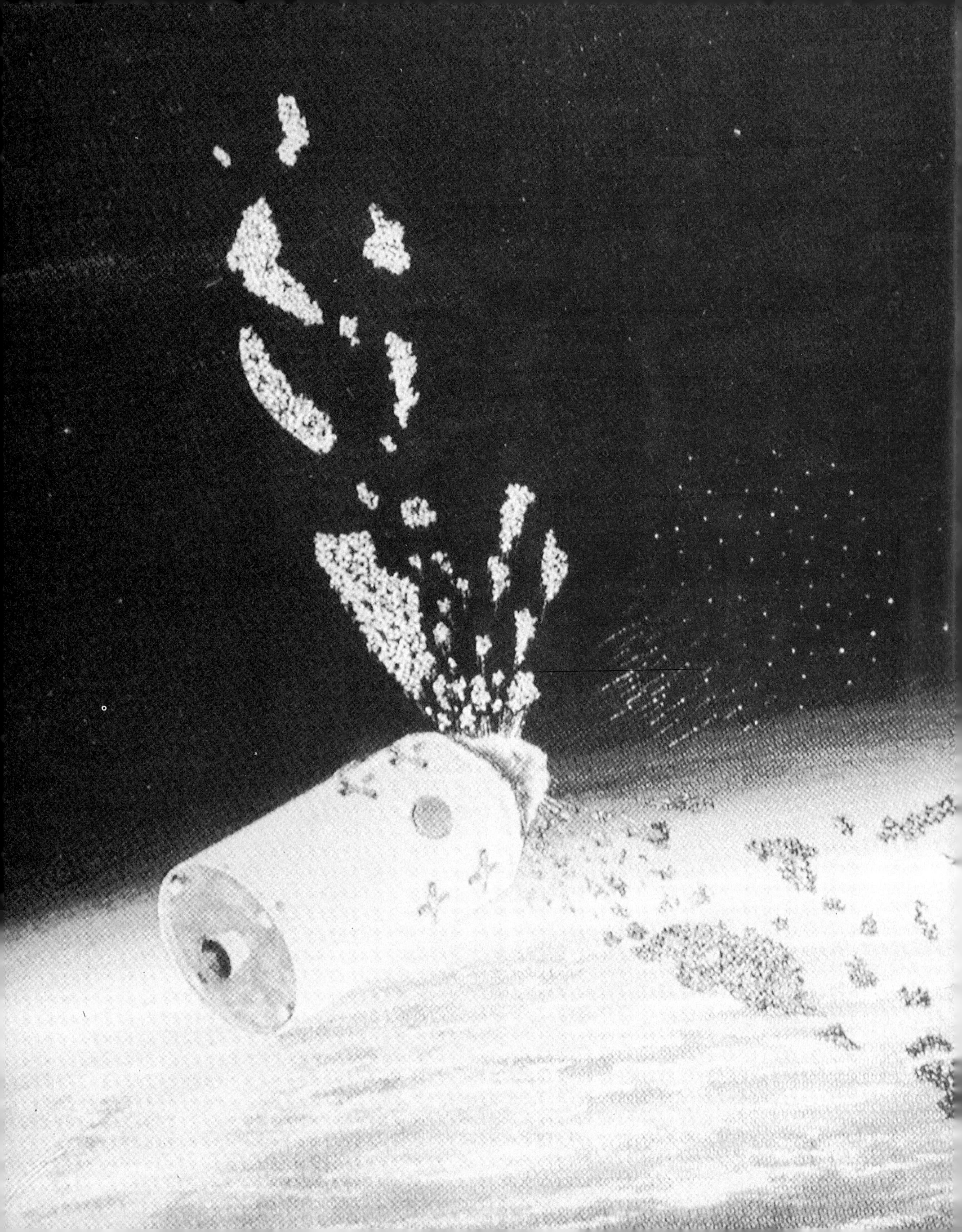

Left: Operational since 1971, this Soviet ground-based antisatellite system is capable of attacking targets in near-Earth orbit using a radar sensor and pellet-type warhead. Several interceptors could be launched each day.

Below: A Titan I booster missile body without explosives or liquid propellant explodes after being irradiated for several seconds with a high-energy laser. This test, carried out for SDI at White Sands Missile Range, New Mexico, served to confirm the vulnerability of missiles.

One line of anti-SDI argument is that it is totally unrealistic in scientific and practical terms – and that Washington, under Reagan, has allowed a newly-found movie fantasy image to run away with itself. However, the SDI advocates – while admitting that certain early public demonstrations were staged – readily explain that this was only to make a difficult concept easy to understand, and that "the real thing" will work. While conceding that SDI might work in the relatively short term, other critics fear that it will usher in a new period of US isolationism.

A further worry is that Washington will stagnate under a defensive umbrella rather like the prewar French behind their Maginot Line – ignoring steps taken by an enemy to penetrate it. Many Europeans, particularly in West Germany, are beginning to believe that any removal of the threat posed by MAD will give the Warsaw Pact the advantage; with its huge superiority in conventional weaponry, the Eastern bloc could gain rather than lose. This European faction will only support SDI if the US Army in Europe is considerably increased.

The US has given her allies the opportunity to participate in the research, which has met with a mixed response mirroring each country's attitude to SDI. There are European demands for a higher share of the high technology work so far offered by the US. Many scientists are also demanding that the knowledge gained by them through research – their intellectual property – be fully disseminated by them. The Pentagon is, however, demanding total control.

While the US is now fully committed to the research on the practicality of SDI, it is far too early to establish whether Star Wars will prove a success. Whatever the problems it faces, whether political, military or technical, SDI will be one of the most expensive projects in US military history. Certainly, the consequences of SDI and the Soviet Union's own research in this field will have a profound effect on the member countries of NATO and the Warsaw Pact in the future.

An artist's impression of a space-based chemical laser antiballistic missile system that would be capable of destroying attacking missiles in the launch phase, before they could deploy MIRVs or decoys.